ALEXANDER YAKOVLEV

Alexander Yakovlev

ALEXANDER YAKOVLEV

The Man Whose Ideas Delivered
Russia from Communism

Richard Pipes

NIU PRESS / DeKalb

The main duty of government is not
to interfere with the people.
ALEXANDER YAKOVLEV

NIU Press / DeKalb, IL

Northern Illinois University Press, DeKalb, Illinois 60115

© 2015, 2016 by Northern Illinois University Press

First printing in paperback, 2016

25 24 23 22 21 20 19 18 17 16   1 2 3 4 5

978-0-87580-494-1 (cloth)

978-1-60909-185-9 (e-book)

Book and cover design by Shaun Allshouse

Library of Congress Cataloging-in-Publication Data

Pipes, Richard, author.

Alexander Yakovlev : the man whose ideas delivered Russia from Communism /
Richard Pipes.

    pages   cm

Includes bibliographical references and index.

ISBN 978-0-87580-494-1 (cloth : alk. paper)—ISBN 978-1-60909-185-9 (ebook)

1. IAkovlev, A. N. (Aleksandr Nikolaevich), 1923-2005. 2. Statesmen—Soviet Union—
Biography. 3. Soviet Union--Politics and government--1985-1991. 4. Russia
(Federation)—Politics and government—1991- I. Title.

DK290.3.I17P57 2015

947.085'4092--dc23

[B]

2015035457

Contents

Contents

Documents

Preface

ALEXANDER NIKOLAEVICH YAKOVLEV (1923–
2005) is the unsung hero of the processes known as
perestroika, or reconstruction, and *glasnost'*, or openness, which between 1989 and 1991 liberated the Soviet Union
and Eastern Europe from the Communist dictatorship. He is
unsung to the point of having not a single biography devoted to
him, although he played a key role in providing the intellectual
stimulus to this process. And the main reason for this deliberate
oblivion is that the Communists, whom he helped to deprive
of power, regard him as their *bête noire*, whereas the reformers
prefer to give credit to the head of the Soviet state, Mikhail
Gorbachev, the subject of nearly 350 biographies.

But there is still a third reason to explain the dearth of Yakovlev
biographies, and it has to do with his political philosophy. The
mature Yakovlev—the man who quit government service in 1991
and lived until 2005—became toward the end of his life a classi-
cal Western liberal who shared none of the traditional Russian
values. A man who could say, "The main duty of government is
not to interfere with the people"[1] rejected the belief of the great
majority of Russians who see the role of the state as directing
its population and protecting it from both domestic and foreign
enemies. The "hands off" role of the state had no place in Russia's
political culture.

Yakovlev was without a doubt one of the important political
figures in Russian twentieth-century history, and as such he deserves far more attention than he has so far received. The purpose of this book is to rectify this injustice and to give Yakovlev
his historical due.

In March 2005 I was invited by Mikhail Gorbachev to at-
tend a conference held in Turin, Italy, called "Twenty Years that
Changed the World." It was organized by the World Political
Forum and meant to celebrate the changes wrought in the Soviet

Union during the five-year tenure of leadership by Gorbachev, which began in 1985. In attendance were numerous international foreign policy experts and leaders.

During one of the intermissions I found myself sitting next to Yakovlev. Suddenly, Gorbachev passed by and, noticing us, said with a smile: *"Ah, liudi proshlogo!"*—literally "Men of the past," but with the connotation "has-beens." My immediate rejoinder was, "How do you know? Perhaps men of the future?" Yakovlev did not react and neither did Gorbachev. Gorbachev's off-hand remark was, I thought then and think today, highly offensive.

Yakovlev has been called "the ideological brains behind perestroika" and its "architect."[2] One of Gorbachev's biographers has this to say about him: "[He] has contributed more to the spiritual and political opening up of Soviet society than any of the other people around Gorbachev, perhaps even more than Gorbachev himself."[3] He has also been designated "the father of glasnost,"[4] responsible for abolishing censorship and liberating Soviet minds. And Gorbachev himself called him a man of "brilliant diplomatic abilities."[5] Such a historical personality surely deserves a full-scale biography.

Yakovlev's life provides a unique instance of a leading figure in the Soviet government turning from an ardent Communist and Stalinist into an equally ardent foe of everything that the Leninist-Stalinist regime stood for.

Richard Pipes
February, 2015

ALEXANDER YAKOVLEV

CHAPTER ONE

Youth*

Y AKOVLEV WAS BORN on December 2, 1923, in the small village of Korolevo near Iaroslavl, a provincial town some 150 miles northeast of Moscow. He was the first child of five, the other four being girls, two of whom died in infancy. His father, Nikolai Alekseevich, had four years of school. His mother, Agafiia Mikhailovna, attended school for a mere three months, following which, at the age of eight and a half, she went to work as a nursemaid; she remained illiterate for the rest of her life. Alexander was sickly in childhood, suffering from scrofula, and was not expected to live. He was taught to read at age five by his grandfather, and then attended local schools, the last of which was four kilometers away from his village; he had to walk this distance back and forth daily through a forest.

The family, poor as it was (it had but one cow),[1] was fully committed to the Communist regime: despite never joining the party, his father was, according to Yakovlev, one hundred percent loyal.[2] For this reason he became the first chairman of the local collective farm.[3] Yakovlev's mother was a staunch admirer of Stalin.[4] His father served in the Red Cavalry during the Civil War. Neither his war record nor his work as collective farm chairman protected him from nearly being arrested in the terrible year of 1937, when victims were chosen not because they had done anything wrong but because they were needed to help satisfy purge quotas. As Yakovlev recalled:

---

* Alexander Yakovlev's cousin, Konstantin Fedorovich Yakovlev, is said to have described Alexander's village childhood in the novel *Osinovskie chudaki* (Iaroslavl, 1973). No copy of this book could be located in any US public library, but thanks to Mr. Evgenii Efremov of Kaluga Province in Russia, I did obtain one. Anatoly Yakovlev, Alexander's son, informs me that the character San'ka in the novel represents his father.

It so happened that [father's] one-time commander of the platoon, Novikov, became military commissar in our Iaroslavl region. He often dropped in on us to imbibe a glass and to recall past campaigns. . . . Once he knocked on our window with his whip; mother was at home.

"Agafia, tell the boss that tomorrow there will be a conference in Iaroslavl. He should come at once."

As soon as father had returned from the forest, mother told him all. He made her recall exactly every word of the military commissar. . . . Father made ready, took something with him and left for the night. . . .

At night, they knocked on our hut. Through my sleep I heard something, some talk. In the morning mother said: they asked for father. They came also the following night. After that, no one came again. And after three or four days Novikov returned. He knocked on the window:

"Agasha, where is the boss?"

"You yourself said that he is in Iaroslavl, at a conference."

"But that is over!"

And he left.

Mother called me and told me to run to the village Kondratovo in another region. There lived my aunt with her husband. . . . There father had concealed himself.[5]

When Yakovlev had finished the sixth grade his mother wanted her son to quit school and go to work in the kolkhoz; she was convinced that if he studied longer he would either go blind or turn into a fool.[6]

In August 1939, when he had learned of the Stalin-Hitler pact, Yakovlev's father told him: "This means war."[7] He spent most of the war and some time afterward as a prison guard. Yakovlev was very close to his father, whom he called "my teacher, the closest friend in life, my unshakable authority." His father never beat him but taught him to work, as well as to choose his own way in life.[8] His parents would die six months apart in 1981–1982.[9]

Yakovlev felt great sentiment for his native village. There are scattered hints in his memoirs that the family home had been three times burned down, once set on fire by the village stove repairer, for which he received money to buy a bucket of moonshine vodka;[10] behind this deed probably were enemies of collectivization. Yakovlev was seven (it was in 1930) when their house was set ablaze, following which they settled in the house of a priest, but this too was set on fire in the middle of the night.[11]

What was left of the village consisted of three decrepit, boarded-up huts, which Yakovlev visited annually:

> Some kind of force pulls me, I don't understand. Yes, probably, and it is difficult to divine this holy mystery. I walk along the site of our charred houses, I seek something, perhaps my childhood, which had gone up in flames together with the houses and my first books. Perhaps I pick up fragments of sad yet still nagging recollections. And every year I stand silently on the soil where rose my village castles with three windows on the street, and await something, await, await . . . [12]

As a result of the fires, the family moved first to Krasnye Tkachi, a village on the road to Moscow, and then again to one called Oparino.[13]

CHAPTER TWO

War

YAKOVLEV GRADUATED FROM secondary school at the age of seventeen in June 1941, just days before the Germans would invade the Soviet Union. In November of that year he was drafted, and, after brief training, was promoted to lieutenant in a rifle platoon. While in uniform, he sent his mother from his salary four hundred rubles a month.[1] On August 6, 1942, in the village of Viniagolovo near Leningrad, he was commanding a platoon of thirty "surly" Chuvash peasants,[2] illiterate men twice as old as he who knew Russian poorly, when he was ordered to charge German positions. This is how he describes what ensued:

> It was planned that we would advance at dawn. But in the morning I saw that the mist was rising from the earth earlier than expected. As a peasant lad I knew that in the shaft of light between the mist and the earth the visibility is excellent, as if everything were brightly illuminated. This is some kind of optical effect. I at once ran over to the neighboring company commanded by Senior Lieutenant Bolotov. He also understood that the attack ought to begin at once. And this could be done: to connect by phone with units—artillery, mortars—to change the plan. . . . Bolotov and I went to the major. He was drunk. . . . We said, "They will mow us down!" And he: "Kids!" So we attacked at a time when the shaft of light between the mist and the earth had already reached our waists. . . . Yes, we burst into German trenches, destroyed their weapon emplacements. But the losses were high. . . . I was wounded on the German site: an officer shot me in the chest

and a sergeant-major in the leg. . . . From there five men carried me out on their hands. . . . Four of them were killed. . . . It was a hallowed tradition of the naval infantry not to leave either the wounded or the dead on the battlefield. The Germans did not take us, naval infantry men, prisoner. But neither did we [take them prisoner]. . . . And when I was in the medical battalion, the commissar of the brigade visited me and asked me to tell him what had happened. . . . I told him. The major was demoted and sent to a penal company.[3]

In the hospital, gangrene set in in Yakovlev's wounded left leg, and the doctors were preparing to amputate it. They had Yakovlev sign a document authorizing the amputation. It so happened, however, that an Armenian physician came by and, having examined him, recommended against amputation; he assured Yakovlev that he would still be able to dance.[4] Yakovlev remained in the hospital for half a year, and on February 4, 1943, he returned on crutches to the village of Krasnye Tkachi, to which his parents had moved. The first person he ran into was his mother: she was carrying buckets from a shed that housed their cow and chickens. When she saw him, she dropped the buckets and, shouting "What am I going to do with you?" burst into tears.[5]

"War is war," he wrote later in life:

Recalling it today, I am prepared to ask forgiveness from those German mothers whose sons, because of my soldier's guilt, were unable to learn what life is. I am prepared to forgive those German soldiers whose bullets made me an invalid for life. But as long as I live I will under no circumstances forgive the crimes of Hitler and Stalin, who sent millions of men to their death. There are no just wars, all wars are criminal.[6]

Yakovlev limped for the rest of his life.

That year he joined the Communist Party, which he then regarded as the "life's truth."[7] He affirms that he was at the time a one-hundred-percent committed Communist and faithful citizen of the Soviet Union. He was an ardent admirer of Stalin: "For me, as for many of my contemporaries, he was both a model and a slogan," he recollected. Marxism, however, aroused in his mind some doubts.[8]

Discharged from the armed services, he decided to resume his education and in September enrolled at the Iaroslavl Pedagogical Institute to study history, presumably to train for a teaching career.

On September 8, 1945, he married Nina Ivanovna Smirnova, of whom, keeping private in typical Russian fashion, he has very little to say, except that she was a student at the Institute, one year younger than he, and that she liked to smile and to dance, winning prizes for her waltzes.[9] After he graduated from the Pedagogical Institute in 1945, the party assigned him to attend in Moscow the Higher Party School. There he spent one year. In November 1946 he was appointed instructor in the Department of Propaganda and Agitation in Iaroslavl, a post he would hold for a year and a half. He was on his way to make a party career as propagandist.

His first doubts about the regime he was serving occurred shortly after the war's end. He was shocked to see train after train, with barred windows, in which ex-Soviet prisoners of war were being brought back home to hard labor camps as if they were traitors. Later he learned that during World War II, 4,590,000 Soviet troops had been taken prisoner by the Germans and their allies.[10] Their subsequent incarceration was the consequence of Stalin's notorious Order No. 227, dated July 28, 1941, which defined anyone taken prisoner by the Germans as a traitor. "I went to the station Vspole and saw weeping women, hoping to meet their husband, brother, father, saw falling from the heated cars paper bundles on which were listed the names of the writer and the address of his relatives."[11] He was deeply dismayed that innocent people were treated like criminals: "I know how people became prisoners. Anyone could become a prisoner of war. Not through his own fault. Lack of weapons, surrounded, wounded. They survived by a miracle, and then they sent them to camp. This was monstrous."[12] There were 1,230,000 such victims, and their treatment as turncoats troubled Yakovlev deeply. He never forgot the sight.

CHAPTER THREE

Khrushchev's Speech

I N M A R C H 1953, immediately after Stalin's death, Yakovlev was assigned to work in the party's Central Committee as an instructor in the department of schools. He felt bewildered by the capital city:

> I had neither acquaintances, nor friends, nor schoolmates. There was no one to consult. The Muscovites had their own problems, they discussed events, reacted to them, and I was as if deaf and blind. I began to read in the newspapers and journals articles about which they argued. At first, I understood almost nothing of what the arguments were about, but gradually I was pulled into the chaotic and nervous life of Moscow, full of anxiety, puzzles, thoughtlessness, reticence, which sowed troubling suspicions.[1]

The most traumatic event in Yakovlev's early Moscow life was Khrushchev's so-called "secret speech," delivered in the Large Kremlin Palace on February 25, 1956—a speech that for the first time publicly acknowledged Stalin's monstrous crimes. Entrance to the Palace was by invitation only. Yakovlev, fortunate to be invited, listened to the speaker from the balcony. He recalled the event:

> Khrushchev on the rostrum. Gloomy, tense. His agitation was apparent. At first he coughed, spoke without much conviction, and then gathered speed. He frequently departed from the text, and his improvisations were still sharper and more specific than the appraisals on paper.

I literally froze, from Khrushchev's very first words about the villainies and crimes of Stalin. How was I then? Young; my faith in Marxist-Leninist teaching, in socialism, had not completely disappeared, I had lived with this faith during the Fatherland War. I had hopes for the promised advent of the earthly paradise. It was only with time that I came to understand how much the spell of the fabulous future fooled and blinded.

Of course, in my mind, as in that of many others, there had stirred some vague doubts, some awkward questions; but I tried to persuade myself that they were not all that important. I chased them away, insofar as the "grandeur" conceived by the party, the reverence for the "wise men of the Kremlin" who knew better than anyone what needed to be done, continued to dominate my consciousness, pushing aside all extraneous thoughts. I felt in my soul an oppressive emptiness, but I was not ready for serious conclusions and even less for actions.

Everything seemed unreal, even that I was here, in the Kremlin, and the words that erased almost everything by which I lived. Everything scattered into small bits, like fragmentation bombs in war. In the hall prevailed a tomb-like silence. One heard neither the creak of chairs, nor a cough, nor a whisper. No one looked at anyone else, whether because of the unexpected that was being said or the confusion and fear which, it seemed, had forever lodged in the Soviet man.

I saw claims that the report was accompanied by applause. There was none. But in the shorthand account Khrushchev's assistants inserted it in the appropriate places, in order to depict the congress's support of the report. . . .

The special meaning of that which was transpiring was that assembled in the hall was the highest *nomenklatura* [members of key governmental and state-industrial positions] of the party and state which, in its majority, had participated in Stalin's villainy. And Khrushchev cited fact after fact, one more terrible than the preceding. They left the meeting with bowed heads. The shock was indescribably profound. . . .

The report turned my soul inside out. The enthusiasm for work began to wane, and at times I felt apathy for everything that was occurring. I began to listen much more attentively to the speeches of the authorities and, unexpectedly, to detect in them a mass of pompous trivialities, lies, pretense. I looked much more vigilantly all around and, breaking through the psychological screen with which I had surrounded myself, noted ever more often the careerism, the lack of principle, the boot-licking, the intrigues of the nomenklatura.[2]

As he would write later, Khrushchev's speech "finished him off."[3] The text of that speech was published in the Soviet Union only in the second half of Gorbachev's rule, after long disagreements and with Yakovlev's encouragement.[4]

After the 20th Party Congress, he wrote,

I lived, essentially, a double life, becoming the slave of tormenting pretense. I adapted, I deceived, while attempting not to lose myself, not to defile myself. I lost the desire to work in the Central Committee. I sought a way out. And I found it—more by intuition than by reason. I felt the necessity to relearn, to reread again all that I had read before, to turn to the original sources—Marx, Engels, Lenin, German philosophers, French socialists, British economists; that is, the theoretical sources of the convictions that I had formed.[5]

He asked to be relieved of his responsibilities and to be allowed to enroll in the Academy of Social Sciences of the Central Committee. He was twice refused, but he persisted and in the end got his wish. He studied in the Academy for two years:

It was in the Academy, studying the original sources, that I came to understand fully the hollowness and impracticability of Marxism-Leninism, its inhumanity, its artificiality, its inherent contradictions, demagoguery, and prognostic fraud. These and other conclusions very successfully healed me of the wounds inflicted by the 20th Congress. I began to perceive that Khrushchev was right, although as yet I did not understand why he had, in effect, raised his hand at the very ideology of constructing a new society. And the deeper I penetrated the theoretical ravings of the "classics of Marxism," the clearer appeared to me the source of the impasse in which the country found itself.[6]

As he told an associate in 1988:

I simply cannot understand why Marx, undoubtedly a most intelligent man, did not see that his theory lacks what is most important: the freedom of choice. Despite the pathos and the declaration of Marxism . . . in his socialism there is no place for the individual, and still less for conditions for the individual's all-around and harmonious development.[7]

In later years, he had this criticism of Marx and Marxism: "Essentially, Marxism is the product of the Victorian era, which perceived no objective limits to man's transforming activity."[8]

History did not agree with Marx concerning many problems. He said that the revolution would occur concurrently in several developed European countries. This did not happen. The revolution took place in Russia, yes, because of an astonishing confluence of diverse circumstances. Marx talked about an absolute and relative pauperization of the proletariat. This did not materialize. He wrote that capitalism is a rotting society, for which scientific-technical and social progress was unnatural. This turned out to be false. He raised a commodity-less utopia. . . . Many of the social institutions that Marx viewed as the source of alienation in fact were and remain fundamental conditions of life, universal principles of human social existence—the state, the nation, language, religion, the monogamous family with a separate domestic hearth, family upbringing of children, professional division of labor, the market, private property.[9]

In spite of the shock of Khrushchev's speech and the doubts it had aroused in him about the regime he was serving, Yakovlev remained a party member for another thirty-five years. That was because he firmly believed that in the Soviet Union a change for the better could only be accomplished with the support and help of the Communist Party and not from outside it. As he would explain in 2001:

> There was a time when I sympathized with the dissidents . . . but I came to realize that the dissidents could achieve nothing. . . . In the end I arrived at one conclusion: this savage regime can only be blown up from within, utilizing its totalitarian spring—the party; making use of such factors as discipline and the century-old education in faith in the General Secretary, the Politburo: once the General [Secretary] says so, then it is so.[10]

This proved to be a sound and successful strategy, but it forced Yakovlev to pretend loyalty to Communism and the Communist regime when he no longer believed in either. As he told two American scholars:

> [You] portray yourself as being for socialism, unity of the party, etc., but everything you do [to advance democracy], you should lie that it is for the sake of socialism.[11]

This deception meant that until he was expelled from the Communist Party in June 1991, Yakovlev had continually to pretend that he was a faithful follower of the party line—a deception that must have been, spiritually, highly draining.

CHAPTER FOUR

Columbia University

Y AKOVLEV'S STUDIES OF socialist theory were interrupted in 1958 by an opportunity to spend a year in the United States under the new Fulbright scholarship program. Of the seventeen Soviet students participating, fourteen were selected by the KGB.[1] Yakovlev and three others, all KGB personnel, were sent to Columbia University. They were housed on the twelfth floor of John Jay Hall on West 113th Street, near Harlem.[2] Yakovlev chose to study the presidency of Franklin Roosevelt and the New Deal, because he saw the relevance of this topic to his own country: as he later put it, Roosevelt had saved capitalism, and the lessons he taught were applicable to the Soviet Union, which faced its own crisis. He also intensively studied the English language, with but moderate success; for he never really mastered it. At the end of their visit, in May 1959, the Soviet visitors were taken on a thirty-day tour of the United States—Vermont, Chicago, Iowa—during which they stayed with American families.[3] These studies exerted a profound effect on him; he came to the conclusion that just as Roosevelt had saved capitalism, so steps had to be taken to save Communism. He came to view perestroika as a Soviet version of the New Deal.[4]

As we will note, Vladimir Kriuchkov, the head of the KGB from 1988 to 1991, persuaded himself that while at Columbia Yakovlev began to work for US intelligence, which was a complete fabrication.

Yakovlev's study of American politics undoubtedly gave him some ideas for perestroika. At one occasion he wrote that "no matter what one's attitude towards the United States, in justice one has to concede that the United States is an effective stabilizer in our restless world, although it often commits irritating mistakes."[5]

There is no evidence, however, that the year spent in the United States rid Yakovlev of his antipathy for that country. He found it a country of "strange contrasts and stupendous paradoxes." He had kind things to say about fellow-students at Columbia: "During the entire time of our studies we felt an unchangingly friendly attitude toward us, Soviet students, genuine and healthy interest in the Soviet Union." But on the whole he found the country perplexing and unattractive. Americans, he discovered, loved to laugh even at matters that were tragic. Everything said or written in the United States about the Soviet Union was false. Something or other robbed Americans of happiness: they were invariably worried. All they cared about was making money. They were racist. They never read.[6] His year in America seems to have done little to assuage his anti-Americanism.

On his return, he was reattached to the Central Committee to work on ideology and propaganda. During the next decade he published a succession of anti-American books (listed below, p. 54). In 1968, Yakovlev was placed in command of a group charged with drafting the new—so-called "Brezhnev"—constitution, eventually promulgated in 1977.[7] This work was interrupted in 1973 when he was appointed ambassador to Canada.

His career in the party was proceeding smoothly, although, as he later stated in an interview, he was not bent on it. When asked "What influenced your choice to occupy yourself with politics?" he replied:

It is an interesting question, no one has asked me about it. . . . In the first place, life at that time was extremely politicized. . . . At that time life was politicized by force. There was constant pressure from above on the conscience, on thought. There was created a whole system of politicizing life. . . .

The second series [of influences] consists of chance. I returned from the war. . . . You understand, we are mentally lazy. Somehow we lacked time to think, we were content with the situation. We considered our life entirely comfortable. We did not consider it necessary to think, but accepted everything on faith. All the more so as at that time they incessantly told us that the government always told the truth. . . .

I returned from the front in '43 on crutches. . . . I enrolled at the institute, where at the first Komsomol meeting they elected me to the Komsomol bureau. I did not expect this: it happened accidentally, it seems to me. I did not even have a notion of this. So I had no desire to move along the party path.[8]

After his return from the United States Yakovlev defended a dissertation dealing with the historiography of US foreign policy. For this work he received in July 1960 the degree of *kandidat nauk*, the equivalent of an American doctorate.

He would revisit the United States in January 1970 with a group of senior Soviet journalists. On this trip he met Ronald Reagan, then governor of California, and Henry Kissinger. He also met Jane Fonda, who warned him that Moscow "did not appreciate the full danger of American militarism."[9] The trip did nothing to change his unfavorable view of the United States.

CHAPTER FIVE

Trouble

A LTHOUGH NATIONALISM WAS the antithesis of Communism, which condemned it, under Stalin and his immediate followers the Soviet regime learned not only to tolerate but to encourage it, finding nationalism's appeal to be much stronger than Communism's. This occurred during and after World War II. Russia was now hailed as the source of all great inventions and the home of the world's great civilization. Reading such encomia in Soviet publications, Yakovlev grew increasingly annoyed.

In November 1972, one month before the country was to celebrate the fiftieth anniversary of the founding of the Union of Soviet Socialist Republics, Yakovlev published—apparently on his own initiative and without party approval—a lengthy article in the prestigious weekly newspaper *Literaturnaia gazeta* (*Literary Gazette*) under the title "Against anti-historicism."*

It was to cause a great deal of commotion and have a profound effect on its author's political career. The editor of *Literaturnaia gazeta* warned Yakovlev that its publication could cost him his job, to which Yakovlev replied: "Possibly, I don't preclude it."[1] Yet, because several prominent figures to whom he had showed it approved, he went ahead with its publication.[2]

The essay had several themes, all loosely connected with anxiety over the survival of the multinational Soviet state due to the rise of nationalism, especially among the non-Russian minorities, and fashionable nostalgia for the old, prerevolutionary Russia.

---

* "Protiv Antiistorizma," November 15, 1972, pp. 4–5. It is reproduced in full in the second part of this book.

To begin with, Yakovlev assailed Igor Zabelin, the author of *Chelovek i chelovechestvo* (Man and Mankind), a book published in 1970. Dazed by Gagarin's pioneering space flight, Zabelin was fantasizing about the future of humanity. One of his predictions was that classes would vanish as all of them, labor included, would convert into an intelligentsia:

> Having removed social obstacles to the broadest spread of technical and scientific knowledge, the achievements of culture, the working class ipso facto prepares its own as well as the peasantry's gradual evolution into the class of the intelligentsia, which in the future is destined to be—for ever and ever!—the sole class of human society. But the sole class is a classless, communist society.[3]

Yakovlev responded to this thesis by arguing that it is prevalent among "bourgeois" Western sociologists like Ralph Dahrendorf, Herbert Marcuse, and John Kenneth Galbraith.

Next Yakovlev turned his attention to contemporary writers who idealized patriarchal village life at the expense of the working class and urban culture. He interpreted this as a reactionary doctrine that implicitly rejected the October Revolution and the leading role of the working class. He then took some swipes at Russian, Georgian, Ukrainian, and Armenian nationalists—all this in a very unsystematic and rather muddled manner. Chaotic and repetitive, the article is hard to follow. Its main targets were the publications *Molodaia gvardia* (Young Guard) and *Oktiabr'* (October).

To a disinterested observer, there was nothing in this essay that contradicted Communist dogma. On the contrary: it was written in classic Communist jargon. "Lenin" and its derivatives ("Leninism," "Leninist") are cited no fewer than forty-five times. And immediately upon its appearance the essay was perceived as perfectly orthodox. Yet it aroused doubts from the outset: it was set in print three times and three times withdrawn.[4] The party organ, *Pravda*, wrote ten days after its publication that the "broad repercussions this essay produced in society were not by accident. Profoundly argued, in a party manner, it clearly and principally asserted the necessity of a precise class and Marxist-Leninist approach to the evaluation of any manifestations of history and decisively refuted attempts at its distortion."[5]

That was also the opinion of Viacheslav Molotov, Stalin's right-hand man: when Yakovlev was introduced to him the following year, Molotov told him it was "an excellent article, correct, necessary. I also note a tendency to chauvinism and nationalism. This is dangerous. Vladimir Ilyich has often warned us against it."[6]

But this was not the view of the party's bosses, who were annoyed that Yakovlev published a programmatic essay without their consent. When Yakovlev met Brezhnev, then head of the party and state, whose many speeches he had written, the latter rebuked him for publishing without his knowledge.[7]

A likely explanation of the party's vehement reaction to Yakovlev's article may have been provided to the *New York Times* by his son, Anatoly:

> The real reason for the banishment to Ottawa was that his father had spoken out in Communist Party circles against "the excessive glorification of Brezhnev." . . . "The article in *Literaturnaia Gazeta* served as a pretext," Yakovlev's son said. "I'm not sure that Brezhnev even read it."[8]

Another possible reason for the furor this article caused is that the fact of unorthodox ideas appearing in print implicitly criticized Soviet censorship.

After the offending article had been discussed in high party circles, including the Politburo, Yakovlev was dismissed from the position of head of the Central Committee Propaganda Department and told that he would have to choose another post. He asked to be assigned as ambassador to an English-language country and was appointed envoy to Canada; the serving ambassador, who had been home on leave and was at the airport about to board a plane for Ottawa, was hastily recalled.[9] Yakovlev was to spend ten years almost to the day in Canada—from July 21, 1973, to July 19, 1983—in what he himself designated as "honorable exile."[10]

CHAPTER SIX

Canada

A FTER A BRIEF stint in a hospital for an unknown ailment, Yakovlev left with his wife for Canada. He soon befriended the eccentric Canadian prime minister Pierre Trudeau, an admirer of the Soviet Union: Trudeau had visited that country in 1952, the last year of Stalin's life, and left it full of admiration for its standard of living![1] He is said to have been "nearly alone among leaders of Western democracies in sympathizing with the Soviet side in the Cold War."[2] After the Soviet invasion of Afghanistan in 1979, when the international community refused to sell grain to the Soviet Union, Trudeau secretly offered it to Moscow through Yakovlev.[3] The two saw a great deal of each other, and in their correspondence the Canadian addressed the Russian affectionately as "dear Sasha."[4] When a second son was born to him in 1973, the year of Yakovlev's arrival in Canada, Trudeau named him Alexander and nicknamed him Sasha, apparently in Yakovlev's honor. Hence it is astonishing that in his autobiography the Canadian statesman makes no mention whatsoever of Yakovlev; the latter's name does not even appear in the index. This omission may well be due to the fact that Trudeau knew of Yakovlev's anti-Canadian book published under a pseudonym after he had returned to Russia.[5]

Yakovlev arrived in Ottawa on July 21, 1973, to assume his ambassadorial duties.

He found the job dull because, as he said, Moscow was only interested in the United States:

> I must say that when I recall my years in Canada I have serious complaints about myself. I conscientiously occupied myself

with all kinds of nonsense, in vain wasted a lot of energy and time on all kinds of paperwork, requests, notes—all for nothing. In the center few took Canada seriously. Everything was concentrated on the United States. . . . I came to realize too late that many of my telegrams did not reach the top but remained on the level of the bureaucratic apparatus.[6]

But he did learn passable English and after a year could dispense with an interpreter.

The time on his hands gave him much opportunity to observe and reflect.[7] The decade he spent in Canada was to exert a profound influence on his thinking. He emerged from the experience a different man.

I intensely studied Canadian life—very simple, pragmatic, permeated by common sense. Why don't we want to shake off the chains of dogma? The answer was plain: the imbecility of the [Soviet] government became ever more obvious.[8]

He witnessed here, for the first time, the advantages of a free, competitive economy, especially in agriculture, the weakest link in the economy of the Soviet Union, but also, and perhaps above all, the benefits of the rule of law:

In Canada, for example, I really learned what the farmer system is. I realized that the farmer works more and better than our kolkhoz worker. And also lives better. I learned with satisfaction how the Canadian judicial system works and, naturally, compared it with ours. More than anything, I was struck by the extent to which people could defend themselves. I was raised in a state where the citizen was a priori guilty for all and toward all—toward the policeman, toward the house manager, toward the party bureau. You have done nothing as yet, and they look on you as upon a transgressor and son of a bitch. And here everything was different. Even if you do something wrong they treat you as innocent until the court proves the contrary. Interesting, I thought; it would be good to transfer this tradition of respect for the human being to our soil.[9]

After a decade as ambassador, Yakovlev became dean of the diplomatic corps in Canada.

A momentous event in Yakovlev's life was the visit on May 16–23, 1983, to Canada of Mikhail Gorbachev, a member of the Politburo and a rising star in the Soviet hierarchy, a visit Yakovlev had conceived and organized. Gorbachev's youth and energy distinguished him from the rest of the Politburo, and it was widely anticipated that he would be chosen the next general secretary.[10] It was not their first encounter: they had met a few years earlier in Stavropol, a meeting Yakovlev remembered but that had escaped Gorbachev's memory.[11] In April 1983, Yakovlev had traveled to Moscow to prepare Gorbachev for his Canadian visit.[12]

On May 20, the two men were scheduled for a joint visit to the farm of the Canadian minister of agriculture, Eugene Whelan. Because of bad weather, the minister was late, and they had an opportunity to engage in serious conversation. There was an instant meeting of minds: both men felt that their country was in crisis, that things could not go on as they were but required profound reforms. According to Yakovlev, Gorbachev told him: "The economy is in decline, agriculture is in ruins. Youth is fleeing the village: only old folks remain there. Salaries are beggarly. We are at an impasse. Everything needs to be changed."[13]

Initially, we sort of sniffed around each other and our conversation didn't touch on serious issues. . . . [But] we took a long walk on . . . Minister [Whelan's] farm and, as often happens, both of us suddenly were just kind of flooded and let go. For some reason, I somehow threw caution to the winds and started telling him what I considered to be utter stupidities in the realm of foreign affairs, especially about those SS-20 missiles that were being stationed in Europe and a lot of other things. And he did the same. We were completely frank. He spoke frankly about the problems of Russia's domestic situation. He was saying that under these conditions, the conditions of dictatorship and absence of freedom, the country would simply perish. So it was at that time, during our three-hour conversation, almost as if our heads had been knocked together, that we poured it all out, and during that three-hour conversation we actually came to agree on all our main points.[14]

Yakovlev later asserted that four-fifths of what was to become perestroika had been articulated on this occasion.[15] As he recalled, "In all these conversations the future contours of the reorganization of the Soviet Union appeared to take shape."[16]

During their conversation Gorbachev hinted that he wanted Yakovlev to return to Moscow to assume an important post in the Academy of Sciences. He turned to Yakovlev, concluding the candid conversation: "Surely you have had enough being here, I dare say, don't you want to be home?"

"It is something I have wanted for a long time," Yakovlev responded at once.

"Listen," Gorbachev continued, "We are discussing the question of the candidacy for the directorship of IMEMO. There are many claimants. Would you take this post?"

"Of course. After ten years, I've had it here."

"What do you think, the Academy of Sciences, Fedoseev, will support you?" asked Gorbachev.*

"I think so. I know Aleksandrov, but it is a nodding acquaintance, but Fedoseev has known me for a long time and well. I've always had normal relations with him."

"All right, we shall see," Gorbachev concluded.[17]

Whelan recalled Gorbachev telling him, before returning home, that the party leadership had decided to entrust Yakovlev with the directorship of IMEMO.[18] But in his memoirs, Gorbachev

---

* P. N. Fedoseev was vice president of the Academy of Sciences.

made no mention of his Canadian talk with Yakovlev, although he alluded to it vaguely on another occasion.[19]

Yakovlev ended his stay in Canada convinced that the Soviet Union had to change, but not by blindly copying foreign models.[20]

How impressed Gorbachev was with his new acquaintance is revealed by the fact that as soon as he was back in Moscow he took steps to bring Yakovlev back home. General Secretary Andropov took some time to consent but eventually did so, and by July 1983 Yakovlev was in Moscow.

> I rejoiced in my return to Moscow like a child. I don't like sappy sentimentality, but when you return home there arises the feeling of rebirth. The air was as if the same, and the sky, and the stars, yet everything was different, altogether different.[21]

Yakovlev did not leave Canada without "exposing" its alleged totalitarian practices. This he did in a booklet called *Bednaia Santa Klaus, ili politseiskie oko Demokratii* (Poor Santa Claus, or the Police Eye of Democracy) which he published in Moscow in 1983 under the pseudonym "N. Agashin."[22] It was a scurrilous treatise that described how capitalism created "its sanitary service—a system of repression, intimidation and terror," how it "brainwashed its citizens," how the United States "tyrannized its neighbor."[23] Hiding behind a democratic façade, Canada was really a totalitarian police state. He concluded his pamphlet:

> Capitalist society at its present stage of development cannot but strengthen its punitive apparatus and expand its functions. The system of preserving economic and political power goes up in price, demanding care and attention from the monopolies. The structure of political inquest and repression becomes ever more comprehensive, more penetrating, more mass-oriented and uncontrolled, imparting to the advanced system of capitalist society a more totalitarian character than before.[24]

In other words, supposedly democratic Canada had all the attributes that the "bourgeoisie" attributed to the Soviet Union. This from a man who twenty years later would claim to have learned with satisfaction "how the Canadian judiciary system was working" and how Canadian citizens could "defend themselves." He later explained that he wrote this work because he was angry at the Canadians for expelling someone from the embassy every six months for purely political reasons.[25] The only explanation for the falsehoods in this book was that Yakovlev had to demonstrate his Communist credentials in order to subvert the Communist system. Even so, it was a poor reward for the friendship the Canadians had shown him. No wonder he published it pseudonymously.

True to his word, on his return home Gorbachev promptly went to work to secure Yakovlev the directorship of IMEMO. At the end of May 1983, Yakovlev received a cable from Fedoseev offering him the post. His appointment enjoyed the support of General Secretary Andropov. As Yakovlev recalled it, within five minutes of receiving the cable he responded affirmatively. He took over the directorship on August 16, 1983.

CHAPTER SEVEN

Back Home

I MEMO—*Institut Mirovoi Ekonomiki i Mezhdunarodnykh Otnoshenii* (the Institute of World Economy and International Relations)—was a prestigious think tank of the Academy, and Yakovlev would direct it for the next two years, during which Gorbachev consulted him constantly.[1] He says that he was very happy in this job.[2] In fact, he almost immediately became Gorbachev's idea man and troubleshooter. And when, a few months later, Gorbachev was appointed general secretary, Yakovlev turned into his right-hand man.

IMEMO was the successor to the Stalinist Institute of World Economy and Politics, which had functioned from 1925 to 1948 under Academician E. S. Varga. It was founded in 1956, during the Khrushchev era, and was charged with supplying the regime with objective and reliable data on developments in Western economies, especially such as could be applied to raise the economic performance of the Communist state. It rejected many of the Communist tenets, including the forecast that capitalism was doomed. IMEMO was something of an anomaly in the Soviet state in that it was charged with providing objective—that is, truthful—analyses of capitalist economies and politics in a society that was totally subject to the views and interests of the Communist regime. For this reason it was often in trouble. From 1966 on, IMEMO had been directed by Nikolai Nikolaevich Inozemtsev, who died suddenly of a heart attack in August 1982. By the time of his death, during the regime of Andropov, the situation at IMEMO began to recall the terrible year 1937 with denunciations and fear.[3]

It is said that under Yakovlev's leadership IMEMO succeeded in recovering from the blows it had suffered in 1982, and the closeness of Yakovlev to Gorbachev, who was acquiring strength, regained for the Institute the shaken reputation of a "brain center" for the study of global economic and international political problems. From IMEMO began to flow a stream of notes and work prepared for Yuri Andropov, Konstantin Chernenko, Mikhail Gorbachev, and other members of the Politburo. After a forced pause, the Institute began to work with renewed energy.[4]

This is how Yakovlev recalled his time at IMEMO:

I could not pretend to the level of professionalism of my predecessors. They spent their entire lives in science and I did so only in snatches. Conscious of this circumstance, I resolved for myself the principal question: not to disturb people in their work, to give them the maximum opportunity for self-realization. . . . The work was facilitated by the fact that behind the Institute stood Mikhail Gorbachev, then the second person in the party. He frequently telephoned me, sometimes consulted me, gave various commissions, which we in the Institute gladly carried out.[5]

IMEMO supplied a variety of reports to the government:

At the request of Gosplan our institute prepared a report titled "What the economy of the USSR will be in the year 2000." . . . We wrote that it would be very bad and explained why. In Gosplan they became impossibly frightened and altogether regretted that they had asked us.[6]

There was opposition. Yakovlev cites incidents of party organs interfering with the Institute's work, accusing it of being anti-Soviet. Under Inozemtsev, two of its members had been arrested on charges of anti-Soviet activity. Even so, Yakovlev considered the time spent at IMEMO the best years of his life.[7] He held this post until July 10, 1985, when he was replaced by E. M. Primakov, whom he had recommended for the job.

The very day after Konstantin Chernenko, the aged and ailing general secretary who had succeeded Yuri Andropov, passed away (March 10, 1985) Gorbachev was chosen his successor. The following day, Vice President George Bush delivered to him an invitation from President Reagan to a summit meeting.[8] Gorbachev requested Yakovlev's reaction. He responded with a memo stating tersely: "A meeting with Reagan is in the Soviet Union's national interest."[9] He went on to elucidate:

> Goals of the meeting: a) to obtain a personal impression of the American leader; b) to give a clear signal that the USSR is truly prepared to come to terms, on the basis of strict reciprocity; c) to communicate to Reagan in unambiguous terms that the USSR will not let itself be manipulated, will not relinquish its national interests; d) it is necessary to show subtly that the world does not end with the USA, and, at the same time not to miss real opportunities in the task of improving relations with the USA because in the next quarter of a century the USA will remain the strongest power in the world.[10]

Yakovlev's encouragement of a Reagan–Gorbachev summit was rather surprising given that only a year earlier he had published yet another virulently anti-American book, in which he had accused the United States of using nuclear weapons to blackmail the world.[11] Later that year he would charge Reagan with transforming the United States into a virtually Fascist state.[12] Gorbachev followed Yakovlev's advice and in November 1985 met President Reagan in Geneva in what was to be the first of their five summit encounters. Yakovlev attended all five. He also attended many of Gorbachev's meetings with other heads of state.

CHAPTER EIGHT

The December 1985 Memorandum[*]

Y AKOVLEV WAS CONVINCED that unless drastic measures were taken to reform it, his country faced major upheavals. These measures entailed, above all, a break with the Communist Party's totalitarian power. "It was my profound belief," he would write in 2003, "that, apart from civil war, there was only one way to prevent the crisis prior to the advent of its acute, perhaps bloody phase, and that was the path of an evolutionary break with totalitarianism—through the totalitarian party, by employing its principles of centralism and discipline and, at the same time, leaning on its critical-reformist wing."[1]

One of the reasons for his concern, although rarely mentioned, was the precipitous decline in world petroleum prices—petroleum being the Soviet Union's main source of hard currency. In 1986, a year after Gorbachev had come to power, the price of a barrel of petroleum fell from $35, which it had fetched in 1980, to less than $10.

At the end of December 1985, Yakovlev wrote on his own initiative a lengthy memorandum for Gorbachev containing some of the salient political and economic recommendations of what came to be known as perestroika, or "restructuring." Like everything he wrote, the memorandum is verbose and disorganized. Ideas tumble pell-mell in a stream of consciousness, important ones alongside subordinate ones. Lenin is frequently cited in support of the author's arguments.

---

[*] This memorandum is translated in full on pages 115–128.

The whole memorandum could have been written in a fraction of the space. Yet the ideas it propounds are most significant, for they outline the principal elements of perestroika.

Its main arguments are the following:

1. Soviet society is disaffected and sometimes looks to "bourgeois" countries for a solution of its problems.
2. The principal problems that the USSR faces derive from neglecting the individual citizen, who should be treated as master.
3. The country's difficulties are embedded in political failures. The party should cede much of its power to the state: "The leading role of the party [should consist] not in substituting for the state and economic apparatuses but in constructive control."
4. Elections should offer genuine choices by providing at a minimum two candidates.
5. Judicial institutions should become truly independent and protect human rights, including the right to property.
6. "There should be a law about human rights and their guarantees, a law about the inviolability of persons, property, and residence, about the privacy of correspondence, telephone conversation, private life . . . the right to demonstrate, freedom of speech, freedom of conscience, freedom of the press, freedom of assembly, freedom of movement."
7. The country should have an elected president, to be nominated from candidates presented by the two parties into which the Communist Party of the Soviet Union should be divided—conservative and reformist—and serve for ten years. The state ought to be administered by an elected general secretary.

It was, indeed, a revolutionary document: nothing like it had been proposed by a high official since November 1917. Most radical was the recommendation that the Communist Party be split, giving Russia a two-party system. But Gorbachev's reaction was curt and negative: he dismissed it as "premature."[2] The new General Secretary believed that what the regime needed was not radical reform but "acceleration," a fresh impulse. It took him some two years to realize that the regime was incapable of changing and take steps to implement some of Yakovlev's recommendations—steps that ultimately led to the collapse of the regime and the dissolution of the Soviet Union.

Yakovlev conceded that originally he too had a "romantic" view of the country's predicament:

> At that time I believed in reforming socialism. It seemed to me that it was enough to remove from it the machine of repression, resting on fear and renowned for its arbitrary decisions, accumulated filth; to cleanse, to remove the obvious absurdities, to move onto democratic rails, to create a parliamentary republic in which the Communist Party would, along with other parties, struggle for power, to attain the right to the diversity of economic activity, the triumph of law—and all would go well.[3]
>
> I began my activity in the higher echelon of power with a principally erroneous evaluation of the historical situation. I still had a genuine faith in the possibility of doing something rational in the framework of the socialist structure. For a long time I cherished the myth that His Excellency Common Sense would, in the end, gain the upper hand over mindlessness and foolishness, that all this evil derived from the folly and the greed of the nomenklatura. From this emerged the concept of the "renovation" of socialism.[4]

According to Yakovlev, the critical moment leading to a revaluation of his thinking occurred on January 27–28, 1987, when at the Plenum of the Central Committee Gorbachev proposed that political posts be made elective, a proposal the nomenklatura rejected out of hand, knowing it would not be reelected.[5] As Yakovlev told a Western historian: "That was when it became clear to me that the system could not be reformed. It had to be broken. . . . At first I thought we could achieve what we wanted to achieve by eliminating the stupidities associated with the Brezhnev version of socialism and allowing people to display some initiative. But it turned out that the system would not permit this. The system is based on fear and the absence of individual responsibility. Any attempt by an individual to use his initiative was bound to shake the system to its foundations."[6]

CHAPTER NINE

Relations with Gorbachev

Y AKOVLEV'S RELATIONSHIP WITH Gorbachev[1] combined friendship and influence with frustration and disappointment. Although for nearly a decade he was in constant and close contact with Gorbachev, in the end he conceded he was unable to penetrate his psyche:

> It is impossible to reach his soul. His mind is an inaccessible fortress. Sometimes I felt that he was afraid to look into himself, to communicate openly with himself, afraid to learn something that he did not know and feared knowing. He played not only with people who surrounded him but also with himself. Played selflessly. Playing was his nature. As a born and talented artist, like an energetic vampire, he always needed a response, praise, support, sympathy and understanding, which served as fuel for his self-esteem and vanity as well as for his creative activities.[2]

Yakovlev thought that Gorbachev was ignorant of Marxism—his knowledge of it was on the level of Stalin's *Short Course*, which he called "a mockery of Marxism, without the slightest relation to it"—but he praised him for his ability to compromise.[3] In his eyes, Gorbachev was a creature of contradictions:

> Gorbachev belongs to that generation of Soviet people in whose psychology, in a striking manner, there combine—even fuse—it would seem, the most contradictory traits: idealism and everyday pragmatism, official dogmatism and practical

doubts, faith and lack of faith, and also mighty sprouts of
healthy cynicism, knitted by society as well as acquired.[4]

During the six and a half years that Gorbachev served as general secretary and president he was in almost daily contact with
Yakovlev by phone or in person.[5] The two men agreed on a fundamental point of principle: that human values were superior to
class values. This Gorbachev affirmed in a talk with journalists
in October 1986, with a bogus reference to Lenin.[6] The idea is
said to have been planted in his mind by Yakovlev.[7] It meant, in
effect, the abandonment of the Marxist-Leninist theory of the
class struggle as the determinant of human history.

Gorbachev was not very generous to his friend and advisor.
True enough, in his autobiography he frequently refers to him,
but always as an executor of his policies, never as a source of his
ideas. Not a word is said about the conversations with Yakovlev
in Canada in 1983 which, according to Yakovlev, marked the beginning of perestroika. In 1989 Yakovlev told an acquaintance
that during the years of working with Gorbachev, he never heard
a single "thank you":

> I didn't even feel any gratitude from him for the fact that the
> idea of perestroika was born in our first conversations in Can-
> ada.... A friendly and trusting attitude—though not without
> some game-playing—such were our private relations. But to
> acknowledge publicly my contribution—never, no way.[8]

Yakovlev especially resented that, despite repeated requests,
he was never invited to speak on the anniversary of either the
Bolshevik Revolution or Lenin's birthday: according to one
Soviet observer this happened because Gorbachev "did not want
Yakovlev to deliver an address whose ideas and format might
overshadow Gorbachev's own efforts."[9]

Even so, when Gorbachev resigned the presidency of the
Soviet Union on December 25, 1991, he did so by agreement
with Yeltsin and Yakovlev.[10]

Gorbachev was very eager to claim exclusive personal credit for the events that transpired in the Soviet Union during the late 1980s, events of world historic importance.[*] In fact, such vanity rather diminished his contribution.

CHAPTER TEN

Glasnost'

I T I S V E R Y difficult for a person not raised under a totalitarian regime, in which all public opinion without exception is controlled, to appreciate the significance of glasnost': it was like emerging suddenly from a dark dungeon to which one had been confined for decades into the bright sunlight. Authors who had been proscribed became available; historical facts which had been distorted were truthfully recounted; and, *mirabile dictu*, the Soviet government allowed itself to be criticized. Glasnost' was nothing short of a cultural revolution without which perestroika could not have been realized. In his speeches to the leaders of media of mass information, Yakovlev insisted that perestroika was doomed to fail "if it does not fully earn glasnost' and creative freedom."[1] In this process Yakovlev, as the secretary of the Central Committee in charge of ideology, played a critical role.

Glasnost' (the word derives from *glas* or "voice") originally meant "publicity" or "openness" and came to be defined as the antithesis of secretiveness. It is an old Russian word that was revived under Gorbachev and associated with *perestroika*: the latter referred to institutional changes whereas *glasnost'* referred to changes in thinking. After seven decades of Communist rule, during which information and thought had been controlled by the party to an extent unknown in human history, both were rapidly emancipated. Books, films, television programs were allowed to circulate and present opinions that previously had been strictly banned. More than that: the public was allowed to criticize the regime and the party governing it: a heady phenomenon that has rightly been called "a cultural revolution."[2] In an interview given a Czech paper in November 1988, Yakovlev said:

Sometimes in our country glasnost' is understood as exclusively a function of the organs of mass information. But this is a very narrow interpretation. . . . It is necessary that all party and social organizations, all state organs, follow the principle of glasnost'. That everyone be informed of their work, that there be nothing hidden from people. . . . Glasnost' has become one of the most active forms of struggle with the bureaucracy and bureaucratic methods, with corruption and abuse of power.[3]

In actual practice it entailed violating virtually every canon of Soviet censorship, which for decades had regulated what Soviet citizens could read, hear, and see. The media now reported on such previously taboo subjects as Soviet abortion practices, suicide and crime, prostitution and drug abuse.[4] Criticism of the Leninist dogma remained out of bonds, as was that of the official history of the Communist Party and the Soviet Union. But suddenly citizens could acquaint themselves with a vast spectrum of literary and visual arts long hidden from their minds, eyes, and ears. It was a breach in the closed world that contributed considerably to discredit and eventually subvert the Communist regime.

After joining the Politburo in June 1987, Yakovlev played a major role in this revolution. His principal responsibilities were the press, information, culture, science, and international affairs.[5] Following his appointment he "became, in effect, the chief ideologue of pere-stroika and the architect of Gorbachev's cultural policies."[6]

A sampling of glasnost' must suffice. In 1988, for the first time in nearly a century, the *History of the Russian State*, appeared—a conservative account by Nicholas Karamzin, originally published in the early nineteenth century. The authorities also authorized the publication of *Zapiska o drevnei i novoi Rossii* (*Memoir on Ancient and Modern Russia*), which Karamzin had submitted to Tsar Alexander I in 1811 and which contained fierce criticism of the latter's liberal reforms.

In 1989 an edition appeared of the works of Peter Chaadaev; this included his *Philosophical Letters*, which questioned Russia's place in history—a work that caused Nicholas I to declare the author insane.

In 1987 the government allowed the publication of Anatolii Rybakov's novel *Deti Arbata* (*Children of the Arbat*), which depicted Stalin as a paranoid killer. In 1988 Pasternak's *Doctor Zhivago* was published in the journal *Novyi mir*, and the following year, Vasily Grossman's *Vsë Techët* (*Forever Flowing*), a work critical of Lenin, appeared in *Oktiabr'*.

That year *Novyi mir* published Orwell's *1984*. In 1988 the authorities permitted the showing of the Georgian film *Pokaiane* (*Repentance*), which had been produced four years earlier but prohibited. It showed the horrors of Stalinism. A remarkable event was the appearance in 1989–90 of Solzhenitsyn's *Gulag Archipelago*, which was followed by the restoration of his citizenship. Yakovlev endorsed the book's publication.[7]

The works of Russian émigrés were made available, among them Nabokov's *Lolita*. Arthur Koestler's *Darkness at Noon* appeared in 1989.[8]

On August 1, 1990, came the Soviet law "On the press and other media of information," by which time press freedom had become de facto reality. Article 1 forbade censorship. It also allowed private individuals to found newspapers.[9] By 1990 one could argue publicly that the Bolshevik coup of November 1917 had been a mistake. Radio jamming of foreign broadcasts ceased. Yakovlev, who was the official responsible for literature and propaganda, said at the 28th Congress of the CPSU (July 1990): "Dozens of artistic creations previously forbidden were published, and in cinemas films were shown that have lain on the shelves for years. Essentially, there began the recovery of creativity—we emerged from the shame associated with the suppression of the artist's freedom."[10]

Among Yakovlev's contributions to cultural freedom must be mentioned his successful efforts to have Andrei Sakharov released from his Gorkii exile.[11]

Gorbachev, who was rather sparing in praise of Yakovlev, conceded that he had rendered "great service" in this respect.[12]

In front of school with cousins, Konstantin and Nikolai, 1932. Alexander is on the right.

In military school, January, 1942. Yakovlev sits in front, third from left.

Yakovlev's parents, September 1976.

With wife and daughter, Natasha.

Columbia University, 1959. Yakovlev is on the extreme right. Oleg Kalugin is second from left. From Oleg Kalugin, *Spy Master* (London, 1994).

In conversation with E. E. Ligachev and Mikhail Gorbachev (on the right).

As Soviet Ambassador to Canada introduced to the Canadian Governor General, 1977.
From *Aleksandr Iakovlev: Svoboda moia religiia* (Moscow, 2003).

Walking with Gorbachev, possibly on Minister Whelan's farm, during their historic encounter, May 1983.

Anti-Yakovlev demonstration in Moscow, February 1991. The sign—"Promakha ne budet"—means "We shall not miss."

Recipient of honorary degree from Exeter University in the United Kingdom, 1993.
From *Aleksandr Iakovlev: Svoboda moia religiia.*

CHAPTER ELEVEN

Need of a Fundamental Break

A S POINTED OUT, Yakovlev conceded that he and Gorbachev had originally thought that the Soviet system was reformable; it needed only modifications that would infuse new life into it. That perception survived for two or three years—his view of the date kept on changing—but in either 1987 or 1988 the two realized that the system was unreformable, that it had to be fundamentally altered:

> Only some time in 1987 did it become definitively clear to me personally that a society built on violence and fear could not be reformed, that we were confronting the complex historical task of dismantling the whole sociopolitical system, with all its ideological, economic and political roots. Already then the necessity of the most profound changes in ideology, of surmounting its myths and utopias, became sharply intensified.[1]

What followed were fundamental institutional changes—among them the creation of the Congress of People's Deputies, an institution in which, for the first time since November 1917, a portion of the deputies were freely elected. This body replaced the Supreme Soviet and had non-Communists among its members. In the elections for the one hundred Communist delegates, Yakovlev did no better than to gain ninety-ninth place.[2]

CHAPTER TWELVE

Role in Foreign Policy

W HILE YAKOVLEV'S ROLE in perestroika and glasnost' is generally known, the same cannot be said of his contribution to Soviet foreign policy, even though it was quite significant. Suffice it to note that Gorbachev called him "one of the closest associates" in formulating foreign policy.[1] At the September 1988 Plenum of the Central Committee, Yakovlev was appointed chairman of the commission concerned with international relations. A general survey of his foreign policy contribution, however, cannot be presented at this time because no one, Yakovlev included, has provided the raw data.

He was the only other person present during Gorbachev's historic encounter with Margaret Thatcher in December 1984.[2] As previously mentioned, he attended all of Gorbachev's summits with Reagan.

It is known that he firmly opposed Soviet intervention in Eastern Europe in the late 1980s when the countries under Soviet control were beginning to become restless. He was dispatched to Berlin and other East European capitals with the message that there would be no Soviet intervention.[3] When, in October 1989, he had a visit from Zbigniew Brzezinski, President Carter's national security advisor, and heard him say that a united Germany would be a strong power, which was neither in Russia's nor America's interest, Yakovlev replied: "All the same, under no circumstances will we send troops into the German Democratic Republic."[4]

He was dispatched to Czechoslovakia to report on disturbances there.[5] On the day when Soviet troops entered the Czech Republic (in August 1968), Yakovlev was sent to Prague to head a group of

Soviet journalists with the mission of supplying propaganda that justified the Soviet military intervention. Yakovlev tried unsuccessfully to avoid this assignment. It was a sobering experience. He returned convinced that Moscow had to support Dubcek.[6]

"The Prague Spring" taught me a great deal. After Budapest and Prague I understood that the Commonwealth was a delusion without a future.[7]

You know, two days after our troops had entered [Prague] I was there. The purpose was ideological. It was necessary to justify the creation of a worker-peasant government. But one thing jolted my mind and emptied it of everything. I suddenly discovered with horror that they did not like us. You see, the plaster casts of Soviet soldiers which were strung up bore such slogans as: "Van'ki, beat it to your Man'kas!" ["Men, beat it to your women!"] When I came to the square where meetings were underway, I saw with what hatred people uttered the words "freedom, independence." And the demonstration of our savagery and stupidity: all this shook me up. I thought: "Lord, what is going on, what are we doing?" . . . And at that time this Czechoslovakia shook me up. As a politician I was very glad that I was there and observed. I was there for five days, saw with my own eyes. These were great days for me, for my inner education.[8]

After he had returned from Prague, Yakovlev briefed Brezhnev on his experiences there. Convinced that the general secretary was quite ignorant of Marxism, he told him that Dubcek's policies were entirely consistent with Marxist doctrine. Brezhnev welcomed this fib.[9]

Yakovlev also played a role in Moscow's relations with the Baltic republics. These countries, incorporated into the Soviet Union by virtue of the Secret Protocol with Germany of August 1939[10] became restive in 1988, after the local publication of this protocol that had previously been kept secret in the Soviet Union.[11] There were demonstrations objecting to Soviet occupation, which in January 1991 turned violent in Vilnius as Soviet troops attacked the local TV station, causing multiple deaths and injuries. Yakovlev visited Lithuania and Latvia in August 1988 and Lithuania again in January 1990. He was firmly opposed to the separation of the Baltic states from the Soviet Union, stating on one occasion in a private interview that if it occurred perestroika would be finished.[12]

He was firmly opposed to Soviet intervention in Afghanistan, which he called "a horrendous error."[13]

Yakovlev also played a prominent role in Soviet arms control policy. At the Reykjavik summit, Gorbachev presented a package of recommendations that tied together strategic and intermediate nuclear weapons, a forward-based system, and strategic defenses. The summit failed because Reagan insisted on developing strategic defenses. Two months after the Reykjavik meeting, in December 1986, Yakovlev submitted to Gorbachev a memo in which he urged that the "package" approach to arms control be abandoned.[14] Gorbachev agreed, and the proposal made possible a number of arms control accords beginning in July 1991 with START I.

CHAPTER THIRTEEN

The 1939 Secret Protocol

O N J U N E 2, 1989, Gorbachev, through the First Congress of People's Deputies, appointed Yakovlev chairman of a commission to study the secret protocol signed in August 1939 between Nazi Germany and the Soviet Union.[1] This document had been known in the West since the end of World War II, but in the Soviet Union it had been kept completely secret and its existence denied, being declared a "bourgeois falsification of history." Indeed, even Gorbachev, upon coming to power, denied the existence of any documents pertaining to this protocol. What seems to have prompted this fresh inquiry was the publication of the protocol in the Baltic press in the summer of 1988,[2] followed by disturbances in the Baltic republics, which had come under Soviet rule as a result of the secret protocol, one of whose provisions assigned them to the Soviet Union. Yakovlev was the first in the Soviet Union to reveal its existence.

The text of the protocol, which had been drafted in Berlin and adopted by Moscow with minor changes, was finally published in the Soviet Union in mid-1989 in a leading historical journal. It read as follows:

1. In the event of a territorial-political reconstruction of the regions included in the Baltic states (Finland, Estonia, Latvia, Lithuania), the northern border of Lithuania becomes simultaneously the border of the sphere of interests of Germany and the USSR. Both parties acknowledge the interests of Lithuania in the region of Vilno.

2. In the event of a territorial-political reconstruction of regions included in the Polish state, the sphere of interests of Germany and the USSR will run approximately along the line of the rivers Narva, Vistula, and San.

3. The question whether it is in the parties' mutual interests to preserve an independent Polish state and what will be the borders of that state can be conclusively clarified only in the course of further political development.

4. In any event, both governments will resolve this question in the manner of a friendly mutual agreement.

5. Concerning southeastern Europe, the Soviet side emphasizes the interest of the USSR in Bessarabia. The German side declares its complete political disinterest in these regions.

6. This protocol is to be kept by both parties in strict secrecy. (Moscow, August 23, 1939. With the authorization of the government of the USSR, V. Molotov. For the government of Germany, J. Ribbentrop.[3])

Yakovlev adopted an ambivalent attitude toward the Nazi-Soviet pact of 1939, approving its non-aggression portion and condemning the secret protocol. According to him, the former was unavoidable in view of what he perceived to be Anglo-French and US efforts to isolate the Soviet Union. The pact demonstrated that the Soviet Union was able to conduct an independent foreign policy. On July 31, 1989, he submitted a report to the Politburo on the 1939 accords with Nazi Germany in which he wrote:

The facts show convincingly that in August 1939 the USSR had no realistic alternative to protecting its national interests than to conclude with Germany the Agreement on Non-Aggression. This was the only way to upset British plans to draw the Soviet Union into a war with Germany without England and France adopting material responsibilities toward the USSR.[4]

He reaffirmed this view in a talk to the Congress of People's Deputies on December 23, 1989: "The leadership of the USSR was obligated to take steps to assure the security of the country, if only to postpone the onset of the war and to use the time gained to reinforce the economy and defense."[5] It was true, he conceded, that the treaty facilitated Germany's conquest of Denmark, Norway, Belgium, and France.

The secret protocol was another matter. It was never shown to the party or its Politburo.[6] He described it as "amoral."[7] The secret protocol "in the juridical sense was primordially an anti-legal document; it represented a deal that expressed the intentions of the physical forces that have signed it." It departed from Leninist principles. It reflected the "inner essence of Stalinism."[8]

Yakovlev seemed to have been unaware that the Stalin-Hitler non-aggression pact, of which he approved, had been responsible for Hitler launching World War II by assuring him he did not face the prospect of a two-front war. Ultimately, the Soviet Union paid the greatest price for it in terms of human and material losses.

CHAPTER FOURTEEN

Attitude toward the United States

O NE ASPECT OF Yakovlev's mindset that is difficult to explain is his lifelong hatred of the United States. In the words of Jeane J. Kirkpatrick, this hostility was "implacable, unrelieved, splenetic."[1] It is puzzling because it ran contrary to his otherwise balanced worldview and his proclaimed passion for liberty ("Liberty is my religion"), of which the United States surely was a leading representative. His program for Russia consisted, basically, of the main provisions of the US Bill of Rights. Yet nothing he experienced—neither the year spent at Columbia, nor his presence at Gorbachev's summit meetings with US presidents, nor the admittedly crucial aid the United States gave the Soviet Union during World War II, would mollify him. It is difficult to find in his voluminous writings a good word about either the American people or their government.

From 1961 onward he published a steady stream of anti-American diatribes: Ideinaia nishcheta apologetov "kholodnoi voiny": amerikanskaia burzhuaziia (The Ideological Poverty of the Apologists of the "Cold War": the American Bourgeoisie) (1961); Staryi mif v novom svete (An Old Myth in the New World) (1962); Prizyv ubivat': amerikanskie falsifikatory problem voiny i mira (The appeal to Kill: American Falsifiers of the Problems of War and Peace) (1965); Ideologiia amerikanskoi "imperii," problemy voiny, mira i mezhdunarodnykh otnoshenii (The Ideology of the American "Empire," the Problems of War, Peace, and International Relations) (1967); SShA: ot "velikogo" k bol'nomu (USA: From "Great" to Sick) (1969); Pax Americana. Imperskaia ideologiia, istoki doktriny (The American Peace: Imperial Ideology, the Sources of Doctrine) (1969); Ot Trumena do Reigana: doktriny i real'nosti nuklearnogo veka (From Truman to Reagan: the Doctrines and Realities of the Nuclear Age) (1984).

A partial explanation of his obsessive hostility to the United States may be found in what he told the American journalist David Remnick:

> Had I not been in the United States and Canada, I would never have written such books about America. . . . But being an impulsive man, when I read newspapers and books criticizing my country, well, this hurt me deeply. For example, I know that I am crippled. But when everyday people tell me, "You are crippled, you are crippled," I get furious! And then I answer back: "You are the cripple! You are yourself the fool!"[2]

He happened to ignore that Americans criticized not the Russian people but the Communist regime imposed on them.

In his memoirs he added another explanation:

> The deliberate exacerbation of my reflections [on the United States] was partly explainable also by the fact that I had not, so to speak, "shaken off" the primitive American anti-Soviet propaganda, which only fostered Soviet patriotism, that is, worked to strengthen Communist ideology.[3]

"The main smithy of war today is the United States," he wrote in 1965.[4] And again the same year:

> In their calculations and plans, the Americans do not rule out unleashing a war against the Soviet Union, if the political and military leadership in the United States perceives the balance of power as favorable to such a solution.[5]

In his view, World War II was barely over when American imperialism resumed its global advance. The country was in the grip of "suffocating chauvinism," whereas the Soviet Union was a "firm advocate of peace politics."[6]

On the US role in World War II he was ambivalent and con-
tradictory. On the one hand he argued that the United States and
the United Kingdom did all in their power first to unleash the
war and then to perpetuate it:

> The ruling classes of England and the United States consciously
> and deliberately participated in the preparation of World War
> II in the hope that the aggression would be directed eastward,
> against the Soviet Union, and, after destroying the country of
> socialism, the other leading powers would only have to reap
> the harvests. . . . In the course of the war they strove to pro-
> long the struggle.[7]

This was routine Communist blather, which Yakovlev seemed
unable to shake off. He conceded later that some of his books—nota-
bly *From Truman to Reagan*—were not "scientifically objective."[8]

On the other hand, he admitted that US and UK aid was essential to Soviet victory:

> As a front-line soldier I maintain that the Red Army rode on
> American "Studebakers," that we fought with American gun-
> powder. After all, the depots of weapons in the west of the
> country had been captured by the Germans, the resources in
> many armaments were in fact exhausted. In good measure we
> were saved by American and partly English aid. . . . I cannot
> cite exact figures, but in some domains we received half of
> what we needed in armaments, and even more, as for example
> in gunpowder and trucks.[9]

Why the United States and Great Britain would deliver vital military equipment to the Soviet Union if they wanted to prolong
the war and "destroy socialism" Yakovlev did not explain.

A year before his death he said the following in an interview:

> My point of view is very simple. Without the second front, if
> one understands by that not only the landings in Normandy

but the contribution of the Allies to military actions as a whole, we would have lost the war. During the first three and a half months of the war, the five-million-strong Red Army was, essentially, smashed: almost one-half of these five million were captured, and the other half perished. That is, the fight was carried on not by the regular army as such but by a militia incorporated into the army. For this reason, the help of the Allies for the attainment of victory was, if not completely decisive, then for the fate of our country certainly decisive.[10]

An inexplicable statement about America and her allies occurs in an article Yakovlev wrote for *Trud* on July 11, 1995, after visiting South Korea.

When I am abroad—I am there quite often—I experience a smarting feeling of annoyance that we are so retarded. In the case of the United States, England, Canada you have a justification—they have known no war for two hundred years. But South Korea is a quite different matter: some thirty years ago it was somewhere in the backyards of Asia. And during this period it has advanced, if not into the twenty-first century, then into the most contemporary level.[11]

Has he forgotten the two world wars and the Civil War, plus numerous local wars, in which the United States had been engaged in the preceding two centuries? One rubs one's eyes in disbelief. The only possible explanation of that puzzling statement is that it was due to careless writing, that what Yakovlev omitted to say was "on their own territory." Now, that holds true of England but not of Canada or the United States. The United States fought Great Britain in Canada in 1812–14, Mexico in 1846–48, and of course itself, in the very bloody Civil War of 1861–65.

One of Yakovlev's sources on the United States was the American academic Seweryn Bialer. Born in 1926 in Berlin, Bialer spent part of World War II in Auschwitz. Having survived the Holocaust, he settled in Poland, where he joined the

Communist police force and became a member of the Polish Workers' Party. In 1956 he defected to West Berlin, and eventually became a professor of political science at Columbia. He was a firm believer in the durability of the Soviet Union.

Bialer first met with Yakovlev on May 20, 1986, and offered him the following insights: The United States strives to achieve military superiority and conducts negotiations about armament control "as a distracting maneuver." It is unable to adjust to US–Soviet parity. Reagan's politics are not only dangerous but threaten disaster. The United States is the most ideological country in the world. It is shielded by an "iron curtain" that deprives it of knowledge of what is transpiring in the Soviet Union.[12] Bialer's two further sessions with Yakovlev, in November 1987 and February 1988, provided equally illuminating insights.[13] They included advice on how to conduct propaganda in the United States.

As to the Cold War, Yakovlev rightly asserted that it began in 1917, meaning when the Bolsheviks seized power and began their efforts to revolutionize the world.[14]

Curiously, he showed no interest in American history or culture: he was content with superficial eyewitness impressions. As a result he never understood what made the United States a truly great power, in contrast to his own country, whose claim to great-power status rested principally on military might. (After joining the Politburo, he learned to his amazement that 70 percent of the Soviet economy was militarized.)[15]

CHAPTER FIFTEEN

Advocating Presidency

Y AKOVLEV WAS RESPONSIBLE for introducing to Russia the institution of the presidency. He first made a proposal to this effect in December 1985 when he suggested that national power be entrusted to a president to be chosen for ten years by an election. He was to have two vice presidents. The president would be chairman of the Union of Communists, of the Politburo, and of the Council of Presidents of the Republic. The idea proved premature and was not implemented.[1]

It was revived in February 1990 when Gorbachev, after some hesitation, agreed to serve as president and asked Yakovlev to address the Congress of People's Deputies on this subject. "I am convinced," Yakovlev said on this occasion, "that the introduction of the post of president of the Soviet Union will give our entire political system the ability to combine in all instances various forms and means of administration, to optimally divide authority as well as synthesize authority, and, above all, to signify the acceleration of the democratic process."[2] On that day, the Congress voted to introduce the office of president.

The creation of the post of president implied the annulment of Article 6 of the 1977 Soviet Constitution, which gave a monopoly on political power to the leadership of the Communist Party. That article read, in part, as follows: "The leading and guiding force of Soviet society and the nucleus of its political system, of all state and public organizations, is the Communist Party of the Soviet Union."

In the words of Gorbachev: "The amendment to Article 6 and the addition of Article 127 to the basic law were organically related. The first meant that our state would cease to be a single-party, even, in a certain sense, theocratic, state, and that one of the main principles of democracy—ideological and political pluralism—would be introduced. The second meant the recognition of a no less important principle of this democracy, namely the separation of powers."[3]

On March 12–15, 1990, the Third Congress of People's Deputies elected Gorbachev president. Gorbachev won the presidency with 1,329 votes for and 495 against.[4]

These events meant that the Communist Party had lost its monopoly on political power and that other parties could legitimately form and function: the Soviet Union became, for the first time since 1917, a country with a multiparty regime.

CHAPTER SIXTEEN

Accusations of Treason

D URING THE FIRST three years of Gorbachev's leadership, the conservative elements in the Communist Party remained largely passive, apparently expecting that, as in the case of Khrushchev, criticism of the regime would be confined to words and not affect their authority. But by the third year, they began to grow restive. The first overt manifestation of their concern was an article in the newspaper *Sovetskaia Rossiia* under the title "I cannot give up my principles," published on March 13, 1988, almost to the day on the third anniversary of Gorbachev's appointment as general secretary. The author was one Nina Andreeva, an obscure teacher of chemistry in the Leningrad Technological Institute, and it is generally believed that behind her stood Egor Ligachev, the leader of the conservative faction of the Politburo. In any event, Ligachev endorsed the article, describing it as in "every respect a remarkable document" and urging that it be distributed nationally.[1] It was probably no coincidence that Andreeva's article appeared at a time when Gorbachev was out of the country, visiting Yugoslavia, and Yakovlev was about to depart for Mongolia.[2]

According to Andreeva, Soviet youth was perplexed. It was being told that Communists "dehumanized" life, and Stalin was blamed for Hitler's rise to power. Stalin's era was distorted, although it had made Russia a great power: even Churchill praised Stalin. The author shared anger at the repressions of the 1930s and 1940s. One of her students "startled her" by saying that "class struggle" and "the leading role of the proletariat" were obsolete concepts.[3]

Yakovlev was put in charge of the counterattack. He responded to Andreeva's article twice: on March 13 (the day he was scheduled to depart for Mongolia) and on March 25 in the Politburo.[4] Publicly, he responded with an unsigned article in *Pravda* on April 5.

Even before Nina Andreeva's article had been published, an open campaign began against Yakovlev, who was widely perceived as the guiding spirit behind perestroika and glasnost'. In June 1987 there appeared a leaflet with the title "Stop Yakovlev!" It warned that Yakovlev was about to replace Ligachev and assume the second place in government.

> Who is Yakovlev? A. N. Yakovlev is the main inspirer of the political course whose ultimate aim is the attainment of detente at the cost of complete capitulation to imperialism.
>
> A. N. Yakovlev is exerting the strongest pressure on M. S. Gorbachev to have him resume diplomatic relations with Israel, for which he is praised to the heavens by the radio station of that fascist state.[5]

Another leaflet charged the Jews with "occupying" the globe and urged that Yakovlev and his allies be killed.[6] A leading source of such publications was the anti-Semitic organization *Pamiat'* [Memory], which accused Yakovlev of being a Jew whose real names were listed variously as Epstein, Yankelevich, and Iakobson.[7] As early as 1986, *Pamiat'* had called Yakovlev the leader of the "Jewish-Masonic" loge.[8] *Pamiat'* even sent scouts to Yakovlev's native village in a vain attempt to confirm that he was a Jew. In Moscow, during the demonstrations in support of the Communist Party and socialism in 1991, demonstrators carried placards provided by the KGB with signs: "Yakovlev is the agent of world Zionism" and "Yakovlev is an agent of the CIA."[9]

These efforts were in part reactions to Yakovlev's sympathy for Jews and aversion to anti-Semitism, attitudes rare among Soviet officials. One of the reasons for the absurd charge that he was Jewish was, as he himself noted, that he was "the only one in the political leadership publicly to condemn anti-Semitism."[10] Anti-Semitism, he once told a colleague, made him physically ill.[11] In his study *Krestosev*, for example, he devoted an entire chapter to Stalin's obsession with the Jews. He described how after Stalin's ascent to power Jews were persecuted and how Stalin promised Ribbentrop to put an end to Jewish "domination."[12] Aware of Yakovlev's Jewish sympathies, Gorbachev once sent him to Kiev to participate in the commemoration of the Nazi Babi Yar Jewish massacres in World War II, in which an estimated hundred thousand lives were lost.[13]

Yakovlev's nemesis during the last year of Gorbachev's presidency was Vladimir Aleksandrovich Kriuchkov (1924–2007), who in 1974 had been appointed head of the KGB's foreign operations and, in late 1988, head of the KGB. Oleg Kalugin, a general in the KGB and subsequently a resident of the United States, wrote of him in his memoir: "In all my years in the KGB, I encountered few members of our organization as scheming, slippery, and duplicitous as Vladimir Aleksandrovich Kriuchkov."[14]

According to Yakovlev, in his ambition to head the KGB Kriuchkov went out of his way to cultivate him: "Kriuchkov energetically sought to befriend me, literally sucked up to me, constantly telephoned me, invited me to the sauna, in all ways depicted himself as a reformer."[15] He portrayed himself as favoring radical reforms and opposing collective farming.[16] Yakovlev brought Kriuchkov to Gorbachev's attention, yet as soon as he was appointed head of the KGB Kriuchkov changed his attitude toward him:

> Of course, supporting his promotion to the post of the KGB chairman I did not expect him to be grateful, but still. . . . It is especially loathsome that literally two or three weeks after his appointment Kriuchkov revealed his true face, openly joining the ranks of the opponents of perestroika, speaking again about "enemies," "agents of influence." In other words he actively began preparations for a state coup, compromising some, blackmailing others, recruiting yet others.*

---

* *Sumerki*, 534. The "state coup" was the unsuccessful attempt in August 1991, which Kriuchkov directed, to remove Gorbachev from office.

Kriuchkov began his campaign against Yakovlev by telling Gorbachev in 1989 that his closest associate was in fact an agent of US intelligence services. According to him, Yakovlev had been recruited by the CIA while a student at Columbia. Kriuchkov repeated these allegations in June 1990. In November 1990, at an official demonstration on Red Square, placards claimed that Yakovlev was an "agent of the CIA."[17] Personally, Kriuchkov came to regard Yakovlev as "one of the most sinister figures in our history."[18] Gorbachev was both surprised and dismayed by this information and took precautions.[19] According to Yakovlev, "he surrounded himself with people who had no honor, who had weak reason, [and] he lost the threads of authority. The leadership of the KGB purposefully fed him lies."[20] Yakovlev now found he was receiving a tenth of the documents he had been given previously and that his phone was tapped.[21] Eavesdropping devices were placed in his office.[22] He felt he was being followed.[23] His son was shot at in a train by an unknown assailant and his daughter's car was set on fire.[24]

Finding that he was being sidelined and unable to gain Gorbachev's support, at the end of July 1991 Yakovlev tendered Gorbachev his resignation. The main reason for this act is said to have been the feeling that he no longer had Gorbachev's trust. "[Gorbachev] attempted to persuade me to stay on, but to this day I have the impression that both Shevardnadze and I had become a burden for him. He succumbed to Kriuchkov's false information."[25]

Kriuchkov continued his anti-Yakovlev campaign and, half a year later, in January 1992, initiated legal proceedings against him on the charge of cooperating with US intelligence. Gorbachev testified at this trial, as did members of the KGB; no evidence of Yakovlev's association with US intelligence was found, and in June 1993 the charges were dismissed.[26] After it had been demonstrated that Kriuchkov's accusations were false, Yakovlev was advised he could sue him:

But I was dissuaded by the general procurator. "Alexander Nikolaevich," he told me, "bear in mind that if you win the suit, he will get five years of jail for slander." And then I thought, "Dear Lord, will I drift to the point where I will be imprisoning people?" And I dropped the matter.[27]

In October 1992 Yakovlev testified before the Constitutional Court, which was trying the Communist Party. A certain Professor F. M. Rudinskii asked him publicly if he was an agent of the CIA. Silence descended on the court room. "'Thank you for the question,' slowly, slowly responded Alexander Nikolaevich. For a moment he froze, tried to recall something, and finally said: 'My masters at the CIA told me you are an agent of Israeli intelligence, but I don't believe it.'"[28]

CHAPTER SEVENTEEN

Bolshevik Crimes

FTER LEAVING GOVERNMENT service, Yakovlev's main preoccupation was with the past, that of his country and his own. On September 28, 1987, the Politburo had created a commission to study materials connected with the repressions that took place from the 1930s to the beginning of the 1950s, that is, in the period of Stalin's dictatorship and to rehabilitate the innocent victims. Its first chairman was M. S. Somolentsev, the chairman of the Supreme Court; Yakovlev served as member. A year later, on October 11, 1988, after Somolentsev had retired, Yakovlev replaced him as chairman.[1] This position, which gave him access to all the documents reflecting both Leninist and Stalinist terror, was for him a shattering experience: it ended whatever respect he still had left for the Bolshevik Revolution and the regime that emerged from it. As he later expressed it, it was the event that most "distressed him as a human being":

> Through my hands passed thousands of cases. Ninety-five percent of them were falsehoods. Sometimes crude, sometimes less so, but still falsehoods. For me these repressions had been a secret. But I was distressed, and this distress, apparently, I will bear with me.
>
> The greatest secret of the party is how it had managed to transform all of us into idiots, denouncers, careerists, people without conscience and honor. This is the greatest mystery. The party knew how to play on the basest instincts. We welcomed murders. How was that possible? Were we all afflicted by some general unknown physical illness? Or were there

some other causes? Why have we turned out to be such a herd? Why did we applaud murders, violence? Why did we readily agree with all that the party said? This is the greatest mystery—political, psychological, moral.[2]

Yakovlev headed the rehabilitation commission for thirteen years (from 1988 to 2001) at no salary. He learned stunning facts, such as that the Soviet regime had shot 300,000 clergymen. In 1938, 42,000 ex-investigators had been arrested, the majority of them subsequently executed.[3] The knowledge acquired as chairman of this commission made Yakovlev into an inveterate enemy of Communism and the Soviet regime.

Lenin now appeared to him as a direct predecessor of Stalin:

I arrived at the profound conviction that the October [1917] coup d'état was a counterrevolution that laid the basis of the criminal-terrorist state of the Fascist type. . . .[4]

It was Lenin who elevated terror into a principle and practice of attaining power. Mass executions and tortures, hostage-taking, concentration camps, including those for children, deportations, nonjudicial repressions, military occupation of one or another territory of Russia—all these crimes began their mindless dance immediately after the October coup. To hang peasants, to freeze clergymen in ice-holes, to suffocate insubordinates with gas—all this could be done only by a monster with an insatiable lust for blood who, with savage obsession, took charge of our fatherland, a maniac who robbed the people of the last crumb of bread, who destroyed thirteen million humans in the civil war.

In other words, the inspirer and organizer of terror in Russia was Vladimir Ilich [Lenin] who forever is to be charged with crimes against humanity.

The history of Lenin's heritage—Stalinism—fundamentally and for the most part hardly conceals the possibility of principally new revelations, except perhaps from the point of view of psychiatry. . . .[5]

As a matter of fact, in his punitive practice Stalin invented nothing that has not been done under Lenin: executions, hostages, concentration camps, and so on. . . . Lenin, Stalin, Hitler, the three creators on neo-Cainism. The main criminals of the century.[6]

It is a lesson that many, indeed most, historians of twentieth-century Russia, have yet to learn.

Yakovlev especially stressed Lenin's role in the persecution and murder of children, a fact generally not known. The Bolshevik authorities took hostage the children of the 1921 Kronstadt rebels and later the offspring of peasants who opposed collectivization. In the postwar resettlement of "disloyal" minority nationalities of some 2.1 million, children under sixteen represented 755,000 of whom 27 percent perished.[7]

As a result of the commission's work, about one million sentences were reviewed and repealed, and more than two million victims of the repressions had their good name restored.[8]

In 2000, Yakovlev published a paperback book under the strange title *Krestosev*, or *The Sowing of Crosses*,[9] in which he detailed the findings of his commission: the persecution of children, socialists, peasants, the intelligentsia, the clergy, prisoners of war, nationalities, Jews, the sailors of Kronstadt. He ended the book with a roster of accusations:

Bolshevism cannot escape responsibility for the counterrevolution, for the violent coup d'état of 1917.

Bolshevism cannot escape responsibility for the establishment of a dictatorship that despised human beings as such. As a result of its criminal activities more than sixty million human beings were exterminated. Bolshevism, a species and forerunner of Fascism, was the principal force that pursued the genocide of its own people.

Bolshevism cannot escape responsibility for unleashing the fratricidal Civil War, which resulted in the destruction of the country. In the course of the senseless and bloody conflicts and devastations, more than thirteen million people were killed, perished from hunger, or emigrated.

Bolshevism cannot escape responsibility for the destruction of the Russian peasantry. Peasant Russia was destroyed; its morality, traditions, customs were repudiated. The productive forces of the village were sapped to such an extent that for many years, to save itself from famine, the country has had to buy foodstuffs abroad.

Bolshevism cannot escape responsibility for the destruction of Christian churches and monasteries, Muslim mosques, Jewish synagogues, other chapels, for the executions of priests, for the persecution of the faithful—actions that have brought the country eternal infamy.

Bolshevism cannot escape responsibility for annihilating entire classes of Russian society—officers, gentry, merchants, the true intelligentsia, scholars, and artists.

Bolshevism cannot escape responsibility for the practice, unheard of in history, of trampling upon elementary rights, for falsifications, wrongful accusations, extrajudicial sentencing, for executions without trial and investigation, for tortures and torments, for the organization of concentration camps, including those for children-hostages, for the use of poison gas against peaceful citizens. In the carnage of Leninist-Stalinist repressions, over twenty million people perished.

Bolshevism cannot escape responsibility for abolishing the freedom of speech, of all democratic parties and movements, including those of a socialist orientation.

Bolshevism cannot escape responsibility for the incompetent conduct of the war with Hitlerite Fascism. Only the sacrifice of thirty million of our citizens and the nation's heroism saved the country from enslavement.

Bolshevism cannot escape responsibility for crimes against ex-Soviet prisoners of war and repatriates, for having driven them after the war into Soviet camps and using them for the harshest labor for the purpose of annihilation.

Bolshevism cannot escape responsibility for waging genocide against non-Russian citizens of the USSR—Germans, Poles, Tatars, Chechens, Ingush, Karachaevs, Koreans, Balkarians, Kalmyks, Turks-Meshketins, Armenians, Bulgarians, Greeks, Gagauz people, who were forcibly resettled from their homelands in uninhabited regions of the country.

Bolshevism cannot escape responsibility for organizing the persecution of scholars, writers, movie-makers, theater producers, musicians, physicians, for the immense casualties inflicted on native culture and science. Criminal motives led to the ostracism of genetics, cybernetics, progressive trends in economics and philology, in literary and artistic creativity.

Bolshevism cannot escape responsibility for organizing racist trials (against the Jewish Anti-Fascist Committee, "doctors-murderers"), intended to inflame dissent among nationalities, to arouse base instincts of the masses.

Bolshevism cannot escape responsibility for organizing criminal campaigns against any and all deviations of thought. The latter's numerous representatives were subjected to the widest array of punishments: prisons, exile, special settlements, expulsion abroad, psychiatric hospitals, dismissal from work, the publication of slanderous articles in the press, and other insults.

Bolshevism cannot escape responsibility for the total militarization of the country, as a result of which the nation became destitute and the development of society was catastrophically impeded.

Bolshevism cannot escape responsibility for the antigovernmental mutiny of August 1991, which resulted in a disorderly breakup of the state and inflicted unimaginable hardship on all nations of the ex-Soviet Union.[10]

Yakovlev estimated the victims of the Bolshevik regime at close to sixty million: thirteen million in the Civil War, thirty million in World War II, fifteen million victims of Stalin's terror.[11] From

1921 to 1953, 5,951,364 citizens were arrested for "counterrevolution"; of these, close to 800,000 were condemned to death.[12]

Impressive as this list of charges is, it misses several other major crimes committed by the Bolshevik regime:

1. The forcible incorporation of a number of non-Russian nationalities into the Soviet Union during and immediately after the Civil War. These facts may not have been known to Yakovlev because they were ignored by Soviet historiography.[13]
2. The Stalin-Hitler (aka Molotov-Ribbentrop) Non-Aggression Pact of August 1939. Yakovlev considered it a necessary step by the USSR to relieve it from the isolation in which the Allies had allegedly placed it, but in fact it unleashed World War II, in which the USSR and the rest of the world would suffer tens of millions of casualties.
3. The 1932–33 man-made famine in the Ukraine and the North Caucasus, estimated to have claimed five million lives.
4. The 1940 Katyn massacre of 22,000 Polish officer POWs.

One of the mysteries that Yakovlev succeeded in solving was the fate of Raoul Wallenberg, the Swedish diplomat who during his residence in Nazi-occupied Budapest in the second half of 1944 saved thousands of Hungarian Jews by issuing them bogus Swedish passports. When the Red Army entered Budapest in January 1945, Wallenberg was detained; he subsequently disappeared. Yakovlev learned that the following month Wallenberg was confined in a KGB prison in Moscow and subsequently executed as an alleged agent of German intelligence.[14] This disposed of the Soviet government's lie that he had died of a heart attack.

Yakovlev emerged from this experience disillusioned with humanity: "When you lower yourself step by step into the dungeon by a ladder seventy years long of the Bolshevik regime, full of human bones and desiccated blood, then all your faith in the human being evaporates like smoke in the wind."[15]

The commission he chaired was responsible for the vindication of some five million Soviet citizens, victims of Stalin's murderous paranoia.[16] In 1988 and the years immediately following, such prominent Bolsheviks as Bukharin, Kamenev, and Zinoviev had their names cleared.

CHAPTER EIGHTEEN

The Dissolution of the Soviet Union

A S THE COUNTRY was being torn apart by nationalistic impulses—by September 1990, thirteen out of fifteen republics had declared some form of sovereignty[1]—Yakovlev was eager to preserve its territorial integrity, but he thought this required a change in the constitution: from a unitary state the Soviet Union should transform itself into a federal state, an "SSG"—*Soiuz Suverennykh (or Svobodnykh) Gosudarstv* (a Union of Sovereign [or Free] States).[2] In this federation, the central government's authority would be confined to defense and foreign policy.[3]

CHAPTER NINETEEN

Private Life

L IKE MOST RUSSIAN officials, Yakovlev separated his private from his public life, and hence little is known of the former. He and his family lived modestly on Alexander Nevsky Street, near the Belorussian railroad station, in a four-room apartment assigned to them in 1967; the family included their son and daughter, and later his wife's mother and their grandchildren. They owned neither a car nor a *dacha* (summer cottage), at any rate, until 1991. He usually worked from 9:00 a.m. to 10:00–11:00 p.m. His one hobby was chess.

Physically he was not prepossessing. The American journalist Gail Sheehy, gave us the following description of him:

> Alexander Nikolayevich has a massive head. His forehead protrudes as if his brain is almost too big for his skull. Deep lines flare above his eyes like lightning flashes. His skin is colorless, his sparse hair black as shoe polish with fringes of white at the ears. When a smile breaks across his habitual poker face, a twinkle of sardonic wit enlivens his eyes, but mostly, all the lines in his face drag downward.[1]

Yakovlev often affirmed that he was an atheist. Asked whether he believed in God, he replied: "No. . . . That is, I believe, but don't know myself in what."[2] Yet on one of his trips to Japan he succumbed to the lure of Buddhism, as expounded by Daisaku Ikeda, whose central idea was "the fundamental sanctity of life." In 1998, Yakovlev published in Moscow a book *Postizhenie* [Grasp] in which he expounded Ikeda and Buddhism.

CHAPTER TWENTY

The August 1991 Coup

I T IS SURPRISING that despite his criticism of the Communist Party and repeated suggestions that the party be split, Yakovlev was kept a member in good standing. The denouement came in mid-August 1991, on the eve of the conservatives' attempt to unseat Gorbachev. On August 15, 1991, party officials in Moscow held a meeting at which they formally expelled Yakovlev from their ranks.[1] The main ground for his expulsion was that he had publicly called for abandoning a principal tenet of Leninism, the party's unity:

> Having verbally covered himself up with the process of society's democratization, the pluralism of opinions, under the banner of perestroika he unfolded a fight against the party from pseudo-radical positions, an attack on the ideological and organizational positions of CPSU, against Lenin and Leninism, he openly led to the schism of the Communist Party of the Soviet Union, by so doing violating the Rules.

Referring to a recent article of Yakovlev's in *Izvestiia*, the party's officials noted that "it speaks of the creation of a new party on the basis of a democratic movement that would unite . . . overt anti-Communists, fractionalists in the CPSU, champions of the society of entrepreneurs who had flourished by the authority of the party and now betrayed it."[2]

On these grounds, Yakovlev was expelled from the CPSU.

Yakovlev was not personally consulted or informed of this decision: he first learned of it from the radio.[3] He immediately penned a response in which—quite unnecessarily—he declared his resignation from the party. "I would like to warn society," he wrote, that in the leading core of the party there has constituted itself an influential Stalinist clique that opposes the political path of 1985, and by so doing, impedes the country's social progress.

The matter is, essentially, that the party's leadership, notwithstanding its declarations, frees itself of the democratic wing of the party, *prepares a social reprisal, a party and state coup d'état*.[4]

The last words referred to a coup that indeed was being planned at the time and that attempted, unsuccessfully, to remove Gorbachev from office. Yakovlev had had for some time an inkling that such a move was in the offing—an inkling, not concrete information—and several times had warned Gorbachev about it; but Gorbachev dismissed such warnings. In April 1991 Yakovlev sent Gorbachev a note from Tokyo in which he wrote: "As far as I am informed, and analysis dictates the prediction, *preparations are underway for a revolution from the right* (i.e., Communist)."[5] But Gorbachev rejected the warning as overly emotional, even panic-stricken: "You, Alexander," he told Yakovlev, "overestimate their intelligence and courage."[6] In his recollections of these days, Gorbachev does not mention Yakovlev's warning but claims that "the logic of the profound reforms did not exclude such a turn of events."[7]

When the coup actually materialized (August 19–21) with several members of the Politburo traveling to the Crimea in a vain effort to persuade Gorbachev to resign, Yakovlev was vindicated. Two events ensued. On July 2, 1991, Yakovlev joined with Eduard Shevardnadze, the one-time Minister of Foreign Affairs, to form an organization called *Dvizhenie Demokraticheskikh Reform* (Movement of Democratic Reforms.)[8] Its objective, according to Yakovlev, was "to consolidate all democratic forces of the country to oppose the right danger, the threat of neo-Bolshevism."[9] On September 19, 1991, he was appointed *Gosudarstvennyi sovetnik po osobym porucheniiam pri Prezidente SSSR* (State Advisor for Special Commissions of the President of the USSR).

Yakovlev was the only person present at the December 23, 1991, meeting in the Kremlin when Gorbachev and Yeltsin negotiated the transfer of power to the new Russian president. Yeltsin wanted to offer Yakovlev a position in his administration, but Yakovlev declined. Instead, he assumed the post of vice president in the Gorbachev Foundation. He held it until he had learned that Gorbachev had been monitoring his private telephone conversations, at which time he resigned to form his own foundation.[10]

In November 1991 he headed an unofficial delegation to Washington, DC, in the course of which he met President Bush. In 1993, he administered the television station Ostankino—a strange appointment in that, by his own admission, he did not watch television.[11] He resigned from this post in March 1995. In 1995, he founded and headed the Russian Social-Democratic Party.

And he published, in the fourteen years from 1991 to 2005, no fewer than fifteen books.

A major publishing venture was a succession of massive volumes of documents in a series called *Rossiia, XX vek: Dokumenty* (Russia, the 20th Century: Documents) brought out, beginning in 1997, under Yakovlev's editorship by *Mezhdunarodnyi Fond "Demokratiia"* in Moscow (the International Fund "Democracy"). The series continued to appear after Yakovlev's death. It was designed in sixty-five volumes, forty of them dealing with domestic issues and twenty-five with foreign affairs.[12] Two of the volumes reproduced Yakovlev's own writings: *Perestroika: 1985–1991* (2008) and *Izbrannye interv'iu: 1992–2005* (Selected Interviews: 1992–2005) (2009). The others—as of 2013 there were thirty-nine of them—dealt with the most diverse subjects: Soviet-Hungarian relations, the Lubianka prison, the 1918 anti-Soviet Iaroslavl uprising, Stalin's deportations, Soviet anti-Semitism, etc.

CHAPTER TWENTY ONE

Yakovlev's Final Thoughts about Russia and Russians

FTER HE HAD left the government, Yakovlev gave much thought to his country's political traditions and reached rather pessimistic conclusions. He felt that perestroika had ultimately failed, and that it did so because of the country's political culture. As he told Dan Rather on CBS in February 1990 about his early plans for Russia:

> All we had to do was to tell people that they are free, that they can do what they want, that they can say what they want, write what they want. But it turned out that most of the people were not so enthusiastic. I think we had underestimated the effect of our past.[1]

He now came to realize that the Bolsheviks not only imposed a new regime on Russia but also exploited the country's cultural heritage:

> Yes, the transition from the violent form of government to freedom, from dictatorship to law, comes to Russia with great difficulty. . . . You understand, the genetic habit of treating arbitrariness as a natural condition of life, the ineradicable longing for a tsar-father, general secretary, or president as a savior and benefactor hangs, to this day, like an unmanageable weight on our legs, panders to laziness, chokes individual initiative, serves as a nourishing soil for the formation of a slavish psychology. We Russians are prisoners, slaves, and victims of Fate, not its masters.[2]

On another occasion he wrote that even after the formal abandonment of serfdom in the middle of the nineteenth century, "the slave mentality" remained in place.[3] Lawlessness, he said in 1995, inheres in Russian genes, as does submissiveness: "Genetically we are slaves. Russia was always lawless and in many ways remains lawless now."[4]

He attached particular importance to the absence in Russia of a tradition of private property, which he saw as the first, indispensable step to freedom.[5] Indeed, he came to regard the restoration of private property as essential to true freedom.[6] "Bolshevism deprived the human being of property. And without it man is a slave."[7] But the absence of property in Russia antedated Bolshevism:

> Russia never had normal private property. Property always belonged to the state, its feudal elite. The absence of private property, especially in land, was the original cause of all of Russia's misfortunes during the span of a thousand years. Without property there is no freedom and no fatherland.*
>
> Recall reforms in Russia. They all ended in failure. [Ivan the] Terrible began well and ended in cannibalism. Alexander I began with Speransky and ended with Arakcheev, Catherine corresponded with Voltaire, ah, how she Voltairized, what freedom-loving games she played, and it is also known how she ended up. And Alexander II, a great reformer, and NEP, and the 20th Congress of the CPSU.

He allowed that perestroika could end similarly.[8]

---

* *Omut*, 2:447. This claim, of course, is not quite correct. The nobility acquired their land in property at the end of the eighteenth century. At the time of the 1917 Revolution, private property in land, housing, commodities, and corporations was prevalent.

CHAPTER TWENTY TWO

Death

I N OLD AGE, Yakovlev's health left much to be desired: he suffered from diabetes, high blood pressure, and a lung disease. He died from pulmonary embolism, the blockage of the main lung artery.[1] According to his wife, Yakovlev returned to his country house on October 19, 2005, from a medical examination at the Kremlin Clinical Hospital feeling fine. He walked up to the bedroom, sat in a chair and died.[2] He was buried at the Troekurovskii cemetery. Surviving him were his wife Nina, son Anatoly (b. 1953), daughter Nataliia (b. 1947), seven grandchildren, and one great-grand daughter.

Putin released a letter of condolence in which he credited Yakovlev with ensuring "the democratic renewal of our country, the development of civil society, and the construction of a state based on the rule of law."[3]

Yakovlev was one of the most accomplished Russian statesmen of the twentieth century and one who did a great deal of good for his country. Indeed, he was the only high official in Russian history to have advocated and in part, successfully implemented, the entire panoply of Western political values: officials elected by their subjects, government staying out of people's lives, an effective judiciary, respect for private property. He was the inspirer of Gorbachev's reforms. No less an authority than Valerii Boldin, Gorbachev's chief of staff, asserted without qualifications as follows: "It is worth remembering that the notion of perestroika with all its components was mainly the work of Yakovlev. Practically all of Gorbachev's speeches were also based on Yakovlev's thinking."[4] For this he deserves to be far more highly honored than, in fact, he is.

Document 1

"Against Anti-historicism"[*]

The approaching fiftieth anniversary of the Union of Soviet Socialist Republics is charged with special significance. This half-century is brilliant proof of the truth that human history develops on an ascending path, in full accord with the objective laws of social life discovered by the great scholars, K. Marx and F. Engels.

The fifty years of the Soviet Union are manifest evidence of the heroism, selflessness, the historical accomplishments of all nations of the great Soviet Union, who have passed in a tight single file along the difficult path of struggle, labor, and victories. Only with united forces was it possible to construct socialism. Only in conditions of creating a new regime could a new historical community emerge—the Soviet nation.

Soviet social science, Soviet literature and art have developed and matured all these fifty years along with the development of the country, always as active, energetic participants in socialist construction. And they have given many profound and subtle examples of solving this complex task—of reflecting and studying the era—on a lofty scientific and synthesizing and artistic level. As in party documents, which have become landmarks of our history, in dozens of generalizing theoretical works and studies, which have already become Soviet classics, in novels, poems and plays, in remarkable films and spectacles that we rightly call popular, our very life has been reflected—stormy, full of revolutionary dynamism, innovative energy, creative might. In the better works of party journalism, science, literature, and art there is a deep understanding of the historical path traversed by our people, with all its hardships, critical moments, its contradictions and conflicts; and from this analysis crystallize those principal,

[*] "Protiv Antiistorizma," *Literaturnaia gazeta*, November 15, 1972, 4–5.

life-giving tendencies that determine life's direction. The people's past, present, and future are illuminated in these works in the light of the Marxist-Leninist world outlook, with the power of talent that serves the working people. Indeed, our country approaches the glorious anniversary of the great Soviet Union with great achievements, not only in the realm of material production but also in the spiritual sphere.

Today the society of mature socialism solves problems unprecedented in their novelty, scope, and character. Hence the complexity and the multidimensional character of the process of development of the mature socialist society. Hence the contradictions unavoidable in all development.

Of course, the complexities and contradictions of social life bear today an entirely different character from past periods of our country's history, now more than half a century old. They are determined by the fact that the Soviet people must solve tasks that—if one is to speak of their scope and depth—have never arisen before.

1.

The socialist present is a difficult but exceedingly rewarding sphere of scientific analysis and aesthetic generalizations, studies and typification. The main concern of social science, literature, journalism has always been the study and reflection of that innovative, progressive, communistic principle that establishes itself in our life. And from this, the degree to which the eyes of the scholar or artist, capable of perceiving the novelty, are far-seeing; the degree to which his heart generously gladdens at the new; the degree to which the progress of his thought is profound in penetrating the future—on all this depends the social significance and buoyancy of the scientific or literary work. The question is to know how to accurately analyze and inspiringly to dream, or, to speak in Maiakovskii's words, "to pin the day to the paper" and to peer into "the Communist far away."

As a matter of fact, the scholar or writer of our time is not simply a man who takes a pen in hand in order to depict an era, either by means of strict scientific conclusions or striking artistic images. In both instances, he is an investigator who analyzes the most complex phenomena and the most profound processes.

To understand the complexity of life's situations and manifestations, to be able to appraise them correctly, to distinguish genuine values from false ones, it is necessary to possess strong class guidelines, ideological conviction, political insight. Equally incompatible with these qualities are dogmatic intolerance, ossification, revisionist omnivorousness, fashionable pseudo-innovation—any departures from scientific, dialectical-materialist methodology, from the Marxist-Leninist principles of analysis. To know how to analyze, from scientific positions, a situation, social conditions in all their complexity and contradictoriness, to perceive the possibility of diverse factors influencing the development of socialist consciousness, to appraise the degree and depth of this influence, and to draw accurate political conclusions—in this lies the essence of the approach to the phenomena of life as taught by Marxism-Leninism.

"The entire spirit of Marxism, its entire system," wrote V. I. Lenin, "demands that each position be viewed a) only historically, b) only in connection with others, c) only in the concrete experience of history." The methodological principles of analysis worked out by Lenin for social phenomena are relevant also for science, literature, and political journalism. In the final analysis, departures from these principles lead to distorted conceptions of social reality, of phenomena of the past and the present. Unfortunately, we still encounter individual incidents of such deviations and distortions. And inasmuch as such faulty judgments are enunciated publicly, on the pages of books and journals, it is necessary to subject them to critical analysis.

Among the urgent problems of contemporary social development, which will be mentioned in this connection, one of the first positions belongs to the social structure of Soviet society. This problem was profoundly and comprehensively examined at the 24th Congress of the CPSU [in 1971]. There is fundamental significance in the thesis worked out by the congress that "the rapprochement of all classes and social groups, the education of the

moral and political qualities of the Soviet nation, the strengthening of its social unity, occurs in our country on the basis of
Marxist-Leninist ideology, which expresses the socialist interests
and Communist ideals of the *working class*." This thesis indicates
the social power that stands at the head of socialist progress. This
power, "social reason and socialist heart," in the construction of
a new socially homogeneous society is the task of the working
class, summoned by history to lead the revolutionary transformations up to the complete disappearance of classes.

Of course, the economic and social accomplishments of socialism, transforming society, also have an immense influence
on the working class—the main motive force and creator of social transformations. Transforming society, the working class
transforms itself as well. This finds embodiment, in particular, in
the appearance of ever new units, in the growth of general and
professional culture, education, social activity, the development
of socialist morality.

But the fact that the working class grows, develops, advances
its culture, masters ever new knowledge, new methods of labor,
naturally does not diminish but, on the contrary, strengthens its
leading role in Communist construction.

However, this apparently obvious truth is not correctly understood by all. Thus the assertions made by I[gor] Zabelin, the
author of *Man and humanity,** that "the working class had come
to power in order to yield in the historical arena to the intelligentsia, the class of the intelligentsia," are, to put it mildly, a
departure from the facts of living socialist reality. In the opinion
of I. Zabelin, the working class has "prepared its own, and also
the peasantry's, gradual evolution into the class of intelligentsia,
which is destined in the future—forever and ever!—to be the
sole class of human society."

This lies in the future. And what of the present? For I. Zabelin,
"There is no doubt that, at present, the leading revolutionary
class (this is a further concrete stage of evolution), the class
that has emerged on the eve of the space age, has become the

---

* *Chelovek i chelovechestvo* (Moscow, 1970).

intelligentsia, the manifold activity of which changes and determines the fates of countries and nations."

But as V. I. Lenin wrote on this topic, the intelligentsia never was and never could become an independent class, because it stood out from the basic mass of the population not by class-defining indicators but by professional affiliation with the sphere of principally mental labor. Moreover, the intelligentsia, like any other social group, cannot become the sole class of society, because this sole class will be society proper, that is, a society without classes. Thus, the claims of I. Zabelin, with his apparent effort to take into account that novelty which is brought into life by the scientific-technical revolution is baseless from the outset.

The 24th Congress of our Party stressed particularly the necessity of further strengthening elevation of the role of the working class in all spheres of productive, economic, political, and cultural life. This natural tendency is brought about by the entire advance of socialist development. "The working class," stressed Comrade L. N. Brezhnev in the Report to the Central Committee meeting, "was and remains the fundamental productive force of society. Its revolutionary spirit, discipline, organization, and collectivism define its leading position in the system of socialist social relations."

It seems that in his discourse I. Zabelin ignores the principal criterion—that of class—and as a consequence inevitably succumbs to scholasticism. The book (and especially the essay "Humanity—what is it for?") is filled with abstract arguments concerning the present and future of the planet—without any consideration of the class struggle that, today, still determines the world's social development. While proclaiming communism to be the supreme, ultimate goal of humanity, I. Zabelin, in fact, ignores the very mass force that is called upon to achieve this goal, and to achieve it despite the fierce resistance of the old world. I. Zabelin focuses his attention primarily on problems he considers common to entire humanity, problems of the scientific-technological revolution, the demographic explosion, man's entry into outer space, etc., in the spirit of nonclass futurological utopia, reflecting on "the conduct of human affairs."

Shunning the social view of mankind's destiny, the author also interprets the scientific-technological revolution in isolation from the social foundations of life. And there emerges a faulty understanding of the role of the intelligentsia as some kind of "leading revolutionary class" that appeared "on the eve of the space age" in order to determine the destiny of countries and nations." Here one perceives not socialism but some kind of abstract society "in general."

As for the assertion about the "leading role" of the intelligentsia as "the revolutionary class," this, alas, is not the author's invention. We mean no offence to I. Zabelin, but this has been discussed for a long time by petty bourgeois social theoreticians.

To begin with, bourgeois ideologists have long cherished the myth about the "disappearance of classes" notwithstanding the preservation of private property, and the myth that the development of contemporary capitalism leads to the reconciliation of classes, "class peace," and general social consent and welfare. Classes are only "temporary" social associations. They supposedly emerge when some social, economic, political processes unite together into one large group. For example, R[alph] Dahrendorf claims that classes are "variable," temporarily organized groupings, involved in one or another social conflict, and empirical social entities.

Incidentally, Dahrendorf's assertion is nothing new. It is based on the point of view fairly widespread in bourgeois sociology according to which social differentiation has, as its basis, for example, an identical understanding of social interests. A similar point of view was once disputed by Werner Sombart, the forerunner of contemporary "theoreticians" of convergence, who argued that a class is formed on the basis of "the conviction of a group of people in their community." It is curious that even Freud tried to prove that, allegedly, the Marxist theory of classes and class struggle was precisely one of the causes of the appearance of actual classes, as a result of the split in the nation that gave rise "to the illusory perception of unity" among separate social groups.

Bourgeois ideologists are particularly hostile to the Marxist-Leninist thesis that the regime of private property is the cause of the antagonistic class differentiation of society. Viewing the working class as a relatively unstable social phenomenon, as a "political" stratum comprising those who acknowledge themselves as workers, bourgeois sociologists claim that "the sum of social strata" making up the working class has nowadays completely lost its anti-capitalist, revolutionary nature. Bourgeois sociologists try to prove that the working class has integrated into the system of state-monopolistic organization. This point of view is most distinctly expressed in the works of Herbert Marcuse. In the book *One-Dimensional Man* he asserted that the worker "integrates with his enterprise," that there occurs "a social and cultural integration of the working class with capitalist society." According to Marcuse, "The new technological world of labor liquidates the negative attitude of the working class toward it. The latter no longer appears as a living negation of existing society." Today, according to Marcuse, the working class no longer differs from the class of entrepreneurs, from merchants and other bourgeois groups because, like them, it too is supposedly interested in the preservation of capitalism.

According to another point of view, in contemporary society, the mission of authority can be performed solely by an elite.

The followers of this conception try to prove that supposedly political history is a struggle only of those social groups that stand at the top of the social pyramid.

At the same time, bourgeois theoreticians treat the popular masses as the average and "worst part of humanity" (Ortega y Gasset), "an inert force that resists the creative minority" (Toynbee). As a consequence of their biological peculiarity, the masses, it is asserted, subconsciously crave to submit to the elite, since the people by nature always possess a "herd consciousness." The elite, on the contrary, possesses a special genetic, that is, hereditary, ability to lead, to subdue the masses. It is endowed with some extraordinary physical and nervous energy that is necessary in order to hold its ground in the struggle with its rivals.

According to bourgeois sociologists, the shift of power from the capitalist elite to the intellectual elite is supposedly a peculiarity of the twentieth century. Presently, the ruling class is said to be composed of the intellectually most gifted individuals, and in this manner, the hierarchy of intellectual talents and the hierarchy of social administration increasingly coincide. According to Galbraith, for instance, at the present time people are increasingly divided not by money but by education, and "precisely in this is reflected the essential class [?—A. Ya.] division of our time."

In the end, bourgeois theories speculate actively on new happenings in the techno-economic life of capitalist countries, under the conditions of techno-economic revolution. These speculations are intended to disorient the revolutionary movement. In the theories of a "single industrial society," "stages of growth," "post-industrial society," and the like, are most fully revealed a vulgar technologism, the hypertrophy of the meaning of technical achievements, and the diminution and even blunt ignoring of the role of the main productive force—the great mass of the working people.

Such are some of the ideas of bourgeois theoreticians, ideas that, in the attempt to impose them on the socialist world, they declare universal.

2.

But let us return to domestic matters. We know that in recent years the growth rate of the socialist scientific and technical intelligentsia has outpaced that of other social groups. This process is not only understandable but also a process governed by law. The quantitative and qualitative growth of the intelligentsia is the direct outcome of the policies of the party, aimed at the all-around acceleration of scientific-technical progress, at the further elevation of the culture and education of the people. It is also well known that the effective work of laboring collectives depends to an enormous degree on the managers and specialists, on their competence, their ability to administer, to make correct decisions, and to objectively evaluate what has been achieved. Yet all this gives no grounds to contrast workers of intellectual and physical labor, and to misinterpret their mutual relations.

If it is completely groundless to deny the leading role of the working class, then it is to the same extent unacceptable also to adopt a nihilistic attitude toward the intelligentsia. Any nihilism of this kind is profoundly alien to the ideology of scientific socialism—and this is understandable—because it can bring nothing to society but discord. It is for this reason that our public opinion has subjected to criticism the article "Zero Point Six" (*Oktiabr'*, no. 7, 1971), the hysterical writings of I. Shevtsov, I[van] Drozdov's book *Subterranean meridian,* and some others. The snobbish denial of the historical role of the working class, equally with efforts to elevate the intelligentsia to the role of "the leading class"—or, on the contrary, as is peculiar to the above-mentioned books, to belittle and denigrate its role—is rooted in the same source, namely the failure to understand the changes occurring in the social structure of society and their main trends, a non-socialist interpretation of socialist progress.

The misunderstanding of the laws of real life or confusion in the face of its complex occurrences has given rise among certain journalists not only to delusions concerning the role of the working class and the intelligentsia under socialism but also to extremes of a different kind—militant apologetics of peasant patriarchalism in contrast to urban culture—universal, in the words of one champion of this point of view, "industrial dance."

This error even found a certain theoretical "cachet" in the concept of "origins" which, for some reason, some unexacting editors have given a "green light." In other articles "origins" are persistently contrasted with "intellectualism," and this contrast is passed off as "the contemporary relationship of urban and rural cultures." The supporters of "intellectualism" are attacked by thunder and lightning, and they are called by no other name than "corrupters of the national spirit."

In the conception of the advocates of the theory of "origins"

---

* *Podzemnyi meridian* (Moscow, 1972).

it is the village—the old one, which exists mainly in their imagination, the old *aul*, the isolated *khutor* or *kishlak*, which, in contrast to the city, preserves the traditions of stagnant life—that is the way of life, the main soul-nourishing basis of all-national culture, of some "national morality." This leads to the cultivation of the patriarchal mode of life, of *Domostroi*˚ morals as the fundamental national value. It is only natural that in such a formulation of the question, socialism and those changes it has wrought on our life during the half-century, the social practice of Soviet society, shaping socialist morality, appear as artificially introduced innovations, as a hardly justified destruction of the customary way of life.

"The peasants are morally the most original national type, the originality [of the peasant—A. Ya.] contrasts with the lack of personality (aggressive or passive) that corrupts the national spirit," proclaims M. Lobanov in his book *Muzhestvo Chelovechnosti* [*The courage of mankind*].

In M. Lobanov's book we encounter concepts that have long set our teeth on edge: "the enigma of Russia," "the heavy cross of national consciousness," the "mystery of the people, its tacit wisdom," "the call of natural wholeness" and, in contrast, "the corruptors of the national spirit." These concepts contain not an ounce of concrete historical analysis. There is no understanding of the elementary facts—that "the national feeling, "the national spirit" of the Decembrists and of Nicholas I, of Chernyshevskii and Katkov, of Plekhanov and Pobedonostsev are incompatible, that in a class society there is not and cannot be one and the same "national consciousness" for all.

The non-historical, non-class approach to the problems of ethics and literature characterizes M. Lobanov's perception of Tolstoy's epic, *War and Peace* (the article "vechnost' krasoty" ["The eternity of beauty"], *Molodaia gvardiia*, no. 12 from 1969). M. Lobanov treats the Patriotic War of 1812 as a period of class peace, of a certain national harmony. M. Lobanov does not accept the ideas of the great French bourgeois revolution:

---

* A sixteenth-century work that guided religious and everyday life.

according to him, the deliverance from them as from something "alien, artificial, forcibly imposed," and the return to the "integrity of Russian life" ensured, in his opinion, "the moral invincibility of the Russian army at Borodino."

How far such assertions are from the truth speaks to the fact that it is to the influence of this revolution, and the Enlightenment philosophy that prepared it, that the better part of Russian society is much indebted for the formation of the advanced ideas of their time, that without this influence it is impossible to imagine the spiritual atmosphere of the age of Pushkin and the Decembrists.

M. Lobanov is no less categorical when dealing with the present day. "At one time, our literature about the village"—he declares—"was active, so to say, in terms of organizational-economic proposals, perhaps recommendations for economic organization. How little such recommendations suit the goals of our literature was shown by the experience of the work of V. Ovechkin, who in his time wrote passionate, persuasive essays whose practical urgency was soon extinguished precisely because of the narrow, practical nature of its agenda."

And so, the essays of V. Ovechkin have lost their actuality. But what is the alternative? Echoing M. Lobanov, L. Anninskii answers the question in the journal *Kodry* (no. 3, 1971). He writes:

From Troepol'skii and Ovechkin, from Zhestev and Kalinin, from the writings of Tendriakov and Zalygin of this period, the prose about the countryside inherited, so to say, "the economic analysis of the human being." The novels and romances of V. Fomenko and E. Mal'tsev, S. Krutilin and V. Semin, F. Abramov, P. Proskurin, E. Dorosh were written. . . . These created a panorama of village life.

Did this panorama acquire decisive success in literature?

No. Of course, it did enter the annals and archives of literature. But the main event did not occur here. It occurred nearby.

Lyrical village tales and philosophical essays of young village writers became the real event. . . . The sober economic manager gave way to the village dreamer, the cunning muzhik, the joker, the eccentric, the sage, the very old man, the custodian of century-old traditions.

If one is to believe M. Lobanov, "Our posterity will judge contemporary literature by the depth of its attitude toward the fate of the Russian village. True values, above all moral ones, always live to see their time. And it is good that our village literature is increasingly saturated with values emanating from the depths of peasant life."

Similar world views are expressed in his own manner in the book of poems *Village Gathering* by V. Iakovchenko. "O Rus'! I love your hoary antiquity. . . . There, the forgotten old church has raised a cross above the belfry, like a hand, as if awaiting a sound agreed upon and avoiding sweeping the heavens. Ah, the old, old, forgotten church . . ."

And while one [of the poets] longs for temples and crosses, another drowns in tears over horses, and a third wails over roosters.

Sighs for rocks, ruins, monasteries fill the selection of poems "Poety Armenii" ["The poets of Armenia"] (*Novyi mir*, no. 6, 1972). The lyrical hero of one of the verses sits at the window and sees trucks carrying horses, "which for thousands of years have hauled and hauled, bearing along the history of mankind on their hardy cruppers, their hoofs hammering out that history." And it seems to him that one must save the past from the present. "How should I save you, horses? All I can do is repress my tears, to give my soul for you . . ."

I. Kobzev, in turn, grieves that "in Moscow one does not hear roosters" and writes: "Sometimes I am consumed by grief: oh, my native land, where have you strayed, Rus', once so merry and sprightly?"

In many poems we encounter paeans to churches and icons, and this is by no means a poetic question . . . "Once one could find refuge in the heavens—an intractable force has cut off for us this path," complains V. Iakovchenko. The sentimentalized rural

Rus' is directly contrasted with the contemporary city. "It is said that soon, very soon, the rural folk will be hoisted to the city floors," grieves V. Iakovchenko. He depicts the city and industry as the image of some kind of abstract "evil" or "iron," which ascended "like an evil genius." "The tongue sang iron, its tongue is evil and sharp. Tear! Hack! Make holes, cut! Such are the laws. Such are the rights. Steel is growing. Iron is growing like gigantic grass. Stop! Fed by the age, you have ripened above mankind and still grow. Still too small, still not enough!"

Truly an apocalyptic vision!

In fact, behind all of this lies an ideological position that is dangerous because, objectively, it attempts to restore the past, frightening people with the "malicious spirit of screaming iron," "the industrial dance," which supposedly kill the national individuality. At the same time, they offer, as an alternative to such "horrors," appeals for "the assimilation of the common people," the quest of eternal, unchangeable morality, the affirmation of faith "in the moral principle . . . independent of all except that it is moral, in faith in the eternal spiritual quality, renewing the person, which, in the Russian cultural tradition, was always called "the conscience."

As is well known, Lenin in his time said: "We do not believe in eternal morality and expose the fraud of all tales about morality." In a number of works he wrote about the historical limitation of the patriarchal peasantry, its downtroddeness, its servility, slave psychology fostered by centuries of forced labor; he revealed the duality of its nature as small proprietors on the one hand, and as toilers on the other. Let us recall with what enormous artistic power and depth this dialectic, this duality of the peasantry's nature was, for example, revealed in the novels of M. Sholokhov.

Whoever does not understand this disputes the dialectic of Lenin's opinion of the peasantry, disputes the socialist practice of reconstructing the countryside. The consequence is the emergence of all kinds of vulgar and objective assertions.

"Presently, we very readily rail at patriarchal culture, and this word has acquired in our practice an admittedly abusive connotation," complains A. Lanshchikov in the article "Land and Progress" (Almanach *Kuban'*, no. 10, 1971). "But here not everything is as simple as may appear at first glance. . . . Speaking about the patriarchal structure, we more often than not forget that it is the embodiment of centuries-old actions, the moral and spiritual experience of the laboring class, that it was precisely this and not another setup that assured this class's tenacity of life in the most difficult historical situations." In the novel *Deer and Ponds,* M. Kochneva asserts: "Even in the darkest times the Russian village was never characterized by a narrowness that would amount to idiocy, and only he who imagines a terrible grey wolf behind every shrub that grows outside the city gate can charge it with idiotism."

In the same novel we read: "All are satraps . . . all are lackeys, all are slaves, hidden and open. . . . A nation of slaves. . . . And didn't our dear Nikolai Gavrilovich [Chernyshevskii] go too far," says one of the heroes of the novel. He is a positive hero and the author's sympathies lie entirely on his side. The polemic is not only with Chernyshevskii but also with Lenin. To prove this we will cite a corresponding passage from Lenin's *On the National Pride of Great Russians*:

> We remember how half a century ago the Great Russian democrat, Chernyshevskii, sacrificing his life to the cause of revolution, said: "Pitiful nation, nation of slaves from top to bottom—all slaves." Open and concealed Great Russians are slaves (slaves in relation to the tsarist monarchy) who do not like to recall these words. And in our opinion these words were words of genuine love of the fatherland, love that languishes as a result of the absence of revolutionary spirit among the masses of the Great Russian population.

By the way, Chernyshevskii did not use the words "open and concealed slaves"—they are Lenin's. And Lenin did not call everyone

---

*   *Olen' i prudy* (Moscow, 1969).

"lackeys," "open and concealed" but only those who were "slaves in relation to the tsarist monarchy."

In this case, whom are our adherents of the patriarchal village fighting, and whither are they calling us?

But never mind the moral values of the past, if even the "traditions" of a gastronomical kind have become the subject of sorrow! According to V. Kozhinov, the loss of national distinctiveness has manifested itself especially keenly among us . . . in relation to food. "Eating, whether in one's family or in company, has been since time immemorial a genuine religious rite and ceremony. It began and ended with a prayer of thanks," writes V. Kozhinov in the journal *Kodry* (no. 3, 1971), drawing further a picture of "Russian eating," with its abundance, beauty and "spirituality," as something nationally special, something linked to "millennial tradition, to the people's tradition." Doesn't all this sound abusive? Following the logic of V. Kozhinov's reasoning, we find the gluttonous Gogol character Petr Petrovich Petukh the most outstanding champion of national traditions. Perhaps one should remind V. Kozhinov with what anger Russian literature wrote about the nobility's gluttony, and with what grief it spoke of Russian villages called "Burnt out," "I went hungry," "Bad harvest" and so on.

Hunger, poverty, shackled peasants, and the lash of serfdom, or, speaking in the language of Lenin, "the slave past," "the slave present," "the great servility"—this is what was inextricably associated with the concept of patriarchal Russia, which the protagonists of "eternal morality," people out of step with history, cherish in their imagination. It is appropriate to bear in mind that V. I. Lenin directly identified the patriarchal way of life with savagery. And there we are to seek moral ideals, the "origins" of moral regeneration!

Let us say at the outset: we favor a cautious attitude toward everything progressive and democratic, toward that which contains the moral experience of nations and which organically supplements our class moral principles. We feel love toward everything that has been preserved in the national character during the years of the revolutionary struggle and with what has enriched its life by the labor of transforming the soil. We cherish the love of freedom of the laboring peasantry, its scorching hatred of the exploiters. These feelings had thrust it into the bands of Razin, into the armies of Emelian Pugachev, called it to fight the tsar and landlords, and in the historical reckoning, brought it into the regiments of the Red Army.

One cannot but feel proud of the talent of the Russian peasantry, its wit, its endeavor to insert into each deed the lively spirit of mastery. We cherish the feeling of love for the soil and native nature, the feeling of community in labor, the sensitivity to the needs of others that inheres in the peasantry. We wish everyone to respond to the slice of bread acquired by the hard labor of thousands and thousands, as does the laboring peasant.

It is these progressive features in the moral makeup of the laboring peasantry that were destined to be established with the triumph of the revolution, and to be enriched with new content. Active socially transforming industry shaped in the village the character of the laboring collectivist, the Soviet patriot, a spiritually rich personality, for whom the world is not only the regions beyond the neighborhood, but the mighty and free Union of Soviet Socialist Republics. Peasant sons today do not graciously worry about the "self-regeneration of the patriarchal spirit" but they transform the soil, storm outer space!

Speaking of the resolute rejection of playing fools over "peasant origins," we denounce just as categorically a cosmopolitan neglect of the people's traditions. Our argument with the partisans of social patriarchalism by no means signifies a nihilist attitude toward the cultural heritage of peoples. Only a peevish skeptic can "fail to notice" that the activity of the Soviet state in the realm of culture is characterized by enormous concern with the preservation and proliferation of the spiritual heritage of all the peoples of the Soviet Union. The state devotes immense resources for the restoration of monuments of architecture, of works of the fine arts.

Let us be candid: it was not the money of the latter-day bearers of God's word that restored Trakai Castle near Vilno, the

Kremlin of Rostov the Great, and the architectural monuments of Samarkand. But we will not pray for every church onion dome and every minaret, and we do not intend to moan over "holy relics" and "wailing walls"!

Let us instead note in passing that the laboring peasantry had never come forward as the bearer of a religious mission. About this more than a century ago Belinskii wrote, ironically, that the peasant treats the icon as follows: "If it suits, pray. If it does not, cover the pots," having in mind the very same "blackened images" before which some zealots of patriarchal antiquity presently freeze on their knees.

Indeed, prominent architects and skilled craftsmen participated in the construction of some churches, investing their labor and talent. But we also know something else: that Orthodox churches, and mosques, and synagogues, and Catholic churches were always ideological centers that defended the powers that be. We do not forget that under the vaults of churches, sprinkled like holy water, abided the bayonets of the chastisers who strangled the first Russian revolution; that from the church pulpit Leo Tolstoy was anathematized; that church bells welcomed the butcher Kutepov,* the hangman Denikin, the bands of Petliura. After all, in the last analysis, even the most "democratic" religion is reactionary, it is the ideology of spiritual slavery. When speaking of respect for historical truth one should not sweeten these bitter truths. They will not be eradicated from the people's memory by any kind of verbal juggling about "the eternal spirit," which home-bred Kulturträgers of Orthodoxy, Islam, Catholicism, Judaism, and other faiths so much care about.

3.

Thus there are two extremes. If in the one instance the scientific-technical progress is made absolute, observed from non-class, "all-human" positions, and the intelligentsia is declared the

---

* Tolstoy late in life rejected the authority of the church which, in turn, in 1901, excommunicated him. Alexander Pavlovich Kutepov (1882–1930) was a leader of the anti-Communist volunteer Army in the Russian Civil War.

leading class of society, then in the second instance both the scientific-technical revolution and the intelligentsia, independently
of their social nature, are anathematized. Despite the apparent
polarity of the positions, marked by global cosmopolitanism in
the first instance and national narrowness in the second, they are
related by a common metaphysical approach to complex happenings and trends. They are also related by the ultimate results
because both ignore not only the leading role of the working
class in the construction of communism, but also the real social
structure of our society, the strengthening of its unity, the policy
of the party directed at the gradual overcoming of the essential
differences between the city and the countryside, between intellectual and physical labor.

The old, patriarchal peasantry has completely and perma-
nently vanished from the scene of history, replaced qualitatively
by a new class—the collective farm, socialist peasantry. The social stratum, once the most numerous that had given birth to
petty bourgeois consciousness, petty bourgeois ideology, has departed into the past.

This prolonged historical shift even today generates echoes of
attitudes that contrarily reflect such drastic revolutionary changes. Along with inheriting and assimilating all that is best, what
was and remains in the laboring peasantry that enters the life of
socialist society, there appear outbreaks of what V. I. Lenin in
his time characterized as "reactionary romanticism." "Under this
term," he explained, "is meant not the desire to restore medieval
institutions, but the attempt to measure the new society by the
old patriarchal yardstick, namely the desire to seek the model
in old usages that in no way correspond to changed economic
conditions and traditions."

The mouthpieces of this kind of "romanticism" are most frequently individual writers who had long broken with the village.
Their melancholy "sobs" express interest in the peasantry—not
the peasantry of today, socialist peasantry, but that of the past,
in that village, to which the present day's urbanite is frequently attached only by memories of childhood or adolescence.

Present-day adherents of patriarchalism, as they go into raptures over the illusory world they concoct all by themselves, defend that in the past of the peasantry's life, which today's kolkhoz farmer has abandoned without any regrets.

To speak more precisely, they are talking not even of the old village, but about that "strong peasant" at whose abundant table there really was performed a religious rite, and the rich icon-case was in good order, and books of "the impious schools" were not kept. Except that such a "well-off peasant" was plainly and clearly called in the village a "blood-sucker." And the fact that his life, his way of life, was demolished together with the sacred places dear to his heart during the revolutionary years— this was done not from malicious intent and ignorance but in full consciousness. They did so in order that in bondage the "well-off peasant" and the one celebrated by the poet as the "sower and keeper" would not suffer but become a citizen enjoying full rights and master of the state of laborers. And the "strong peasant" had to be destroyed. Such is revolution, the inexorable force—it pulls down everything that rises against humanity and freedom.

The key to the understanding of the present time is the consistent class and party position in the evaluation of the past, of the experience of preceding generations. The party has always attached, and presently attaches, serious significance to the correct, objective interpretation of our country's history. As is well known, at the 24th Congress of the CPSU certain attempts to make judgments from non-class positions of the historical path of the Soviet people, to belittle the significance of its socialist conquests, were subjected to justified criticism. At the same time, the party revealed the failure of the dogmatic notions that ignore those major positive changes that have taken place in the life of society.

The party and the literary press have already criticized individual articles in the journal *Molodaia gvardiia* in which the cultural heritage was scrutinized in the spirit of the theory of a "single stream." Moreover, the matter came to the point, as a matter of fact, that such reactionary figures as V. Rozanov and K.

Leontev were idealized and praised, while, on the other hand, representatives of revolutionary democracy were treated with scorn.

The ignoring or underestimation of Lenin's teaching about two cultures in every national culture in regard to the past remains also today one of the manifestations of a non-class, non-social approach to history. To call things by their name, sometimes attempts are undertaken to substantiate the revision of one of the fundamental principles of Marxism-Leninism. Thus, L. Ershov and A. Khvatov, authors of the pamphlet *Leaves and roots*, in direct contradiction to Lenin, proclaim the October Revolution "the great Russian national revolution." They claim that allegedly after October, Lenin nearly revised his theory of two cultures; that after the revolution, in Lenin's attitude to the heritage "there was much that changed cardinally." This does not correspond to reality, because both before and after the revolution Lenin, with full confidence, demanded not non-class omnivorousness but the "development of the best models, traditions, results of existing culture from *the position* of the worldview of Marxism and the conditions of life and the struggle of the proletariat in the age of its dictatorship." The authors of the brochure, alas, assert something different—that, "the culture of socialist society arises not only from consistently democratic elements but also from elements of the cultural stock of the past."

When the clear demand of Lenin, obligatory in an approach to history, is ignored, then the concrete appraisals of some other prominent figures of the past are also distorted. The critic O. Mikhailov, in the journal *Nash sovremennik* (no. 4, 1969), and the prose writer I. Shukhov, in the journal *Prostor* (no.1, 1972), depicted in a clearly romanticized manner the tsarist general Skobelev, ignoring his reactionary mindset and role in the suppression of people's movements in Central Asia. Without any basis whatsoever, M. Kochnev, in the previously mentioned novel *Deer and Ponds*, attempts to challenge the perception of the historian Karamzin as a defender of autocracy and to depict him as our "ideological ally," "a comrade-in-arms" who deserves no more, no less than "national appreciation, national affection."

When one deliberately idealizes the past, in addition to equivocal social positions, then there ensues the absurd controversy over which tsar was the best, while the merits of one or another historical figure are inflated to superlative degrees. One example comes from an article published in the journal *Literaturnaia Gruziia* (no. 8, 1970): "In Georgian history, the name of Queen Tamar is surrounded by a special halo." "The radiant person of Queen Tamar, her victorious reign, her farsighted policy and acumen—today it has become already apparent to everyone— facilitated the political and cultural flowering of Georgia. All this also won her the nation's love, thanks to this the nation composed hymns in honor of its glory—the Queen Tamar . . . Tamar, in the judgment of the nation, was such a good and kind ruler that people dreamt of becoming her subjects."

In the novel *Mech Areia* [*The Sword of Ares*], Ivan Bilyk, attempting to glorify as much as possible the mythical Kievan prince Bogdan Gatilo, went so far as to declare that supposedly under this name appeared Attila, the ruler of the Huns.

Similar attempts at idealization can be noted in some works about Timur, Tsar David, about the movement of Kenesar Kasymov,* about Moldavian cultural figures of the past century, about the history of the Kirghiz state, etc. Need one demonstrate that any hyperbole in such matters can turn into a starting point for the revival of nationalistic prejudices! Hence it is appropriate that these phenomena have received suitable critical appraisal from the party organizations of the republics.

The acclaim of the achievements of "one's" own princes, feudal lords, tsars, by no means serves the task of patriotic upbringing. It takes us back to the servile habit, which was long ago ridiculed by M. E. Saltykov-Shchedrin, of confusing the concept "fatherland" with that of "Your Excellency," and even preferring the latter to the former. Excessive admiration for the past inevitably smooths out class contradictions in the history of this or that nation, conceals the antagonism and irreconcilability of

---

*   1802–1847, Khan of the Middle Horde in Kazakhstan who sought to separate Kazakhstan from Russia.

progressive and reactionary tendencies, dulls vigilance for the contemporary ideological struggle.

One more example: the anthology *O, Russian Land!* In this book, whose purpose, as told in the afterword, is to acquaint our youth with "verses of lofty civil tone, of lofty patriotic and revolutionary fervor," is published without commentary a poem of the prominent Russian poet of the first half of the past century, N. M. Iazykov, "Not to our kind," in which appear the following lines: "You, the insolent and impertinent folk, you, the foolhardy bastions of the teaching of the godless school, you are not Russians!"

To whom is this poem addressed, who were the "not our kind" of people? They were A. I. Herzen and his comrades. The poem itself is a widely known action in the ideological struggle that in its time elicited protests from V. G. Belinskii, N. A. Nekrasov, and A. I. Herzen himself, who called this poem "a police whip" and "a denunciation in verse."

In the same collection, also without commentary, are published the works of other Slavophile poets who glorify autocracy.

It is unlikely that the compilers and editors of this collection did not know all this. Then what is it all about? Is it possible that by the concept "high patriotic and revolutionary pathos" they want to combine the incompatible—revolutionary democrats and reactionary Slavophiles?

Nevertheless, that which N. Iazykov said with verses already in 1844 was, in a certain sense, repeated by our contemporary M. Lobanov, in the year 1969, though in a non-poetic form. He writes: "The spiritual and cultural displacement of original Russia, her national uniqueness, by a new 'Europeanized' one, standardized like Western countries—this has grieved many profound minds of Russia. Russia is either original, summoned to tell the world her word, or else she becomes, on the Western model, facelessly bourgeois."

As is known, the theme of the homeland, Russia, the concepts of patriotism and love for the fatherland, constituted throughout the nineteenth century an arena of very acute ideological-political struggle. At that time, the ideas of democracy and enlightenment were fundamentally counterpoised to the pillars of reaction and the "back to the soil" movement.

As is well known, anti-Communism, in the search for a new means of struggle against the Marxist-Leninist world outlook and the socialist regime, attempts to galvanize the ideology of *Vekhi*, the ideas of Berdiaev and other reactionary, nationalistic, religious-idealist conceptions of the past, which were shattered by V. I. Lenin.* A vivid example of this is the stir aroused in the West by the works of Solzhenitsyn, and especially by his most recent novel, *August 1914*, which follows *Vekhi* in its philosophy and the Constitutional-Democrats in its politics—a novel that foists on the reader a negative attitude to the very ideas of revolution and socialism, denigrates the Russian liberational movement and its intellectual-ethical values, idealizes the life, the mores, and the customs of autocratic Russia.

Of course, Solzhenitsyn's novel is a manifestation of overt hostility to the ideals of the revolution and socialism. It goes without saying that for Soviet writers, including those whose erroneous views are criticized in the present article, the behavior of the latter-day Vekhovite is alien and offensive.

But something else is clear as well, namely that even simple flirtation with reactionary-conservative traditions of the past, traditions that harken back to the interests and the ideology of the overthrown classes, calls for decisive objections to the ideological unscrupulousness in questions of this kind.

4.

We favor a solicitous attitude toward the cultural heritage, including national traditions. And, of course, the upbringing founded on traditions, especially those born of the revolution and socialism, is an inalienable component of the party's ideological activity.

The rejection of tradition in general is the other extreme of

---

* *Vekhi* [*Landmarks*] was a book written by several authors, published in 1909, which criticized the Russian intelligentsia.

the petty middle class which, as is well known, has many faces. Petty bourgeois consciousness has numerous shadings—from attachment to the canons of *Domostroi* to anarchist slogans like "No authorities!" Characteristically, all these conceptions are completely detached from real sociohistorical practice and, in essence, are nothing more than a jumble of judgments of *pochvenniki* [members of the back-to-the-soil movement] and Slavophiles, to be sure, slightly modernized and "seasoned" with the high-flown imperatives in the spirit of abstract humanism or left-wing ideas of the rebellion of "all and sundry."

For us, the notion of "socialist personality" is indissolubly bound up with proletarian internationalism and the hatred of the laboring for class enemies, for all the remnants of the past. And such a personality is formed only in the process of active, energetic participation in the common job of creating a new world. It is also indisputable that the theory and practice of Communist morality constantly develop and enrich themselves with new generalizations and new experience. Therein lies their vitality and social activism.

The petty bourgeois, according to his objectively given world view (to be a small shopkeeper by persuasion it is not necessary to stand by the shelves of one's own shop) is terribly frightened by the ideological commitment, by organization, responsibility, and other demands that socialist society makes on the individual. The petty bourgeois is accustomed only to make demands on himself and on these demands to construct his philosophy.

In this light we cannot agree with certain assertions made by G. Batishchev in "The tasks of the upbringing of the new human being," in the collection *Leninism and the dialectic of social development*. Let us begin by noting that in this article there is not a word said about the programmatic goals of the party in the formation of the new personality, about the activity of the CPSU in this realm, about these actual tasks of education, which are resolved by the Soviet school, the Komsomol, and society as a whole. It is useless to seek any kind of serious formulation of the problems of education raised by life. The author sees the main

objective of education in "an active and critical image of life."
But again, all "activity," according to Batishchev, reduces itself
to bare criticism, to wholesale rejection. For example, he fiercely
turns against traditions, asserting that people cannot be educat-
ed on that basis. "It [tradition—A. Ya.] is always limited in one
or another way because of its non-creative nature." Yet who is
not aware that revolutionary, military, and laboring traditions
have become an integral part of the sociomoral experience of
our nation?!

As for socialist society, one of its characteristic features is
a high level of organization, conscious discipline. It is these
demands that acquire special relevance at the present time,
at the current stage of both social development and scientific-technical revolution. But G. Batishchev thinks differently.
He writes: "It would be the most harmful nonsense to repre-
sent socialism as a society that establishes yet another type of
routine 'taboo,' customs, dogmatized norms, and ceremonies
consolidated once and for all." Of course, "dogmatized norms,"
if by this is meant conservatism and routine, are harmful. But
should one not remind readers that the concepts "norm" and
"dogma" are not synonymous, and that the humanitarian
principles of socialism serve man only when they are reliably
fenced off from anyone's infringements, when everyone ob-
serves them? Otherwise society will not in any way differ from
Pomialovskii's *"bursa."**

Good traditions will always live, proliferate, reflecting the creative history of the people. Those who, from a lively interest in
the fatherland's past, its revolutionary and cultural conquests,
out of concern for the preservation of the monuments of olden
times, deprive it of any class content, render to the cause more
harm than good—the cause, which, it would seem, they jealous-
ly defend. It is well-known, after all, that the best way to compromise anything that is basically useful is to reduce it to the absurd.
This is precisely what some writers are doing.

Here is a brochure by S. Semanov, *"Russia's Millennium"*

---

* Nikolai Gerasimovich Pomialovskii (1835–63), *Ocherki bursy* [*Seminary Sketches*].

Monument in Novgorod. Of itself, the idea of such a publication arouses no doubts: the monument Russia's Millennium, for all the differing attitudes to it of the progressive-minded forces of Russian society in the past, even today maintains its historic value. But the ambiguity of its fate requires from the contemporary interpreter the utmost accuracy of judgment.

Unfortunately, the author of this brochure did not assume a dialectical stance, one steeped in historicism; he did not take the trouble to separate what is imperishable, from the point of view of art, from the superficial and transient, although it doubtless stands to reason that it was his task to help the reader to understand the ideological nature of celebrating in 1862 the millennium of Russian statehood, which is indisputably reflected also in the design of the sculptor, M. O. Mikeshin. In the words of S. Semanov, the 129 sculptures of the monument reflect "the civic convictions" of their creator, "his understanding of the fatherland and native history."

In reality, the choice of historical figures for the monument bore a severely consistent, tendentious character and expressed not so much the "civic convictions" of the sculptor as the demands of Russian tsarism's official ideology, in the spirit of the threefold formula "Autocracy, Orthodoxy, and Nationality."[†] The pamphlet contains not one shred of social analysis, controversy, or criticism. It gives the impression that the author fully agrees with the concept of "the fatherland's fate" that is reflected in the bas-reliefs and sculptures of the monument.

Everything that the author finds necessary to say about the ceremonial inauguration of the monument, which had been conceived and realized as an undisguised ideological action of autocracy, bears a detached character. "Novgorod has long not seen such a gathering of distinguished guests. Here came Tsar Alexander II, the court, high officials and officers. The celebrations were splendid."

---

[*]   S. Semanov, *Pamiatnik "Tysiachiletie Rossii" v Novgorode* (Moscow, 1970).

[†]   This triad was officially promulgated in 1833 during the reign of Nicholas I by Minister of Education Sergei Uvarov, as the basis of Russia's political culture.

Contemporaries greeted this event in a far less lyrical fashion. A. I. Herzen responded in *The Bell* with an article-pamphlet titled "Jubilee," which expressed a genuinely democratic perspective on the ceremonies, a different concept of the fatherland's destiny and native history. "We are offended by the perpetuation of lies about the past," wrote A. I. Herzen; "we are offended by this bas-relief of fraud. There is something mean-spirited and narrow-minded in the premeditated distortion of history by royal command."

To people unversed in politics and history such a position may appear as some kind of innovation, a "bold" view of events devoid of any bias. But there is a tendency here, and it is quite obvious: carelessness in dealing with real historical facts for the sake of subjectivist, non-social concepts. It is appropriate to recall that some time ago, in the article "Illustrations to a scheme," written jointly with N. Startsev (*Novyi mir*, no. 12, 1966), S. Semanov undertook to "embellish" the politics of Kerensky, asserting, for example, that "after the February Revolution the legal and economic condition of workers improved; an increase in the real wages was achieved." It is as if there had been no execution of the July 1917 demonstration, nor the imprisonment of Bolsheviks in the Kresty prison, nor the murder of the worker Voinov,* nor preparation for the physical elimination of V. I. Lenin. As concerns the "improvement of the economic condition of workers" by the efforts of Kerensky & Co., by the testimony of the Food Committee of the Provisional Government itself, the supply of bread to Moscow and Petrograd workers in September 1917 consisted of less than one-half pound a day, and real wages fell by almost one-half. (Cf. *Istoriia Grazhdanskoi Voiny v SSSR*, vol. 1: 357, 358).

Disregard of social and class criteria can sometimes be observed not only in historical scholarship, but also in literary studies. Take, for instance, the article by B. Egorov titled "Slavophilism," in *The Short Literary Encyclopedia*. Having described in detail the views of the Slavophophiles on the widest range of questions, the only topic for which the author found no

---

* I. A. Voinov, a collaborator in *Pravda*, was killed on July 19 (July 6 Old Style), 1917, for distributing this paper.

space was the characterization of the class roots of this conservative ideology, ignoring, in fact, what is most important—that it reflected the mindset of nobles and landowners.

———

The motives of "neo-*pochvennichestvo*" are not as harmless as may appear on superficial reflection.* If one looks at our life attentively, if one analyzes the dynamics of socioeconomic and moral-psychological shifts in society, then the conclusion is inescapable: social development has by no means wiped out and could not wipe out the distinct borders that separate the national from the nationalistic, the patriotic from the chauvinistic. Something else occurs: the filling of patriotic emotion with a new, internationalist content, its evolution beyond the limits outlined by national origins. In our socialist conditions, patriotism and internationalism in no way contradict each other: they are organically fused, bound into one.

Of course, from the fact that our society has established brotherly cooperation and friendship among the nationalities, that in it dominates an international ideology, it does not at all follow that at present the problems of the patriotic and international education of toilers have automatically been resolved. The actuality of these problems is emphasized in the documents of the 24th Party Congress, in the resolution "On the preparation for the 50th anniversary of the formation of the USSR." Party documents, resolutions of the Central Committee of the CPSU indicate anew the importance of intensifying the internationalist education of the working people, the importance of struggling against the survivals of nationalism, the necessity of a consistent conduct of a strictly scientific class approach to the evaluation of the history of the nationalities.

5.

* *Pochvennichestvo* was a literary and social movement of the 1860's that sought to merge the intelligentsia with the common people.

The sphere of relations among the nationalities in general and, in particular, in a multinational country like ours is one of the most complex issues of social life. And as long as nations exist, one cannot remove from the day's agenda the problem of educating the people of diverse nationalities in the spirit of profound mutual respect, of irreconcilability with the manifestations of nationalism in any of its forms—be it local nationalism or chauvinism, Zionism or anti-Semitism, national conceit or national isolationism.

Bourgeois propaganda strives in every way to rekindle the nationalistic mood. It is well known how active a campaign has been waged by our class enemy in connection with the fiftieth anniversary of the multinational Soviet state. One of the main theses of this campaign is that the Union of Soviet Socialist Republics is supposedly not an organic but rather a purely mechanical union—by no means a mighty union of equal nations who voluntarily chose the path leading to the construction of a new society and united in one socialist family. It is easy to understand how assiduously the slightest manifestations of nationalism are sought and blown up, with what readiness recurrences of petty bourgeois national narrow-mindedness and conceit are picked up, even the most trivial ones.

The party has always been intransigent toward everything that might hurt the unity of our society, including any nationalistic infections, no matter from where and from whom they might emanate.

One such infection appears in reflections about the non-class "national spirit," "national feeling," "national folk character," "the call of native unity," which appear in some articles marked by an objectivist approach to the past. Their striking peculiarity is the detachment of present-day social practice from those historical changes that occurred in our country during the years that followed the Great October; the disregard or incomprehension of that decisive fact that in our country there has emerged a new historical community of people—the Soviet nation. The authors of these articles virtually avoid such words and concepts as "soviet," "socialist," "kolkhoz." For instance, the literary critic V. Petelin suggests, instead of the Marxist formula regarding the essence of man as "a totality of social relations," his own primitive versions: "the essence" of man "in the nationality to which he belongs" (*Volga*, no. 3, 1969). It is as if there exists or can exist in our country some kind of national character outside the decisive influence of the revolution, socialism, collectivization, and industrialization, outside the cultural and scientific-technical revolution, outside the basic social constants of time!

If one tries to drive to their logical conclusion such reflections—by no means shimmering with novelty—then the following obtains: there are in the world no classes, social strata, or groups; there are no ideological trends conditioned primarily by class and social interests; there exist only immutable, unchanging national features, which came into being in unknown times according to unknown laws.

A similar non-social, non-historical conception of the nation and national culture taken as a whole is contrasted with Western European culture, also without taking into account its social differentiation. And a similar contrast is presented sometimes as almost a struggle against bourgeois ideology. However, it is the bourgeois ideologists who depict Russia in her stagnation and backwardness as something contrasted to Europe. They deliberately refuse to see social demarcation and class struggle not only in prerevolutionary Russia but also in the countries of contemporary Europe and America, the existence there of democratic traditions, the spread there of a proletarian, Marxist-Leninist ideology.

Is it necessary to prove how false it is to depict the historically unavoidable and progressive process of the internationalization of the life of Soviet nationalities as the liquidation of national originality! The Communists reject the bourgeois formulation of the question according to which internationalism is conceived as a bare rejection of everything national. As Lenin has said, the international is not the un-national.

"Is the feeling of national pride alien to us, Great Russian conscious proletarians?" asked Lenin. And he responded: "Of course not! We love our language and our fatherland, we work, above all, to raise *its* laboring masses (i.e., nine-tenths of *its* population) to the conscious life of democrats and socialists. We know and feel most of all to what violence, oppression, and humiliation is subjected our beautiful fatherland by tsarist butchers, gentry, and capitalists. We are proud that these brutalities have evoked resistance in our midst, in the midst of Great Russians, that precisely *this* environment has produced Radishchev, the Decembrists, the revolutionary-commoners of the [18]70s." Such is the theoretical foundation of our own, Soviet patriotism, growing out of the revolutionary, democratic, genuinely national traditions of native history, out of the feeling of pride in a nation that has carried out the grandest socialist revolution in the world, that has been the first in human history to construct socialism.

As concerns the individual zealots of the "national spirit" and patriarchal antiquity, they express a certain vestigial consciousness. Such are the attempts to embellish, to whitewash, some representatives of bourgeois nationalism revealed in a number of publications about Ukrainian bourgeois nationalists, about Georgian Mensheviks, Social-Federalists, Armenian Dashnaks. The Tbilisi City Committee of the Communist Party of Georgia, with full justice, has criticized the work of U. Sidamonidze titled *The historiography of the bourgeois-democratic movement and the victory of the socialist revolution in Georgia (1917–1921)*[*] for ignoring distinct class criteria in approaching the problems of Transcaucasia's national evolution. The same holds true of the party publications of Armenia in regard to A. Mnatsakanian's book *Lenin and the resolution of the national question in the USSR.*[†]

It is always useful to remember that the danger of petty bourgeois nationalism is that it paralyzes the sacred feeling of love for one's fatherland, the lofty idea of patriotism, distorting it until it is unrecognizable. As a result, national pride is replaced by

---

[*]   *Istoriografiia burzhuazno-demokraticheskogo dvizheniia i pobedy sotsialisticheskoi revoliutsii v Gruzii (1917–1921 gg)* (Tbilisi, 1971).

[†]   *Lenin i reshenie natsional'nogo voprosa v SSSR* (Erevan, 1970).

national conceit and patriotism turns into chauvinism.

If one looks at matters realistically, then it is fully acceptable that many of the views we have subjected to critical analysis can be regarded, on a personal basis, as a kind of subjective reaction to one or another of the present time's acute problems. But the point, as Lenin has stressed in a well-known letter to A. M. Gorkii, is that the concrete political results of one or another advocacy are determined, in the last analysis, not by "saying 'good' and 'nice,'" not by showing the "truth and the justice," but by the objective social content of the expressed opinions, by the real circumstances of social life.

We know, we value and love many artistic and journalistic works permeated with great pride in one's nation, in its achievements, with pain over its difficult past and joy over its present. Such works are dear to every Soviet person.

As for certain manifestations of anti-historicism, they, of course, in no wise shake the foundations, the principles of Marxist-Leninist analysis, whether of the past or of the present. So much the less are they able to overshadow that wholesome process of strengthening the friendship of nations, the great attainment of revolutionary October, of the socialist system. But one must point them out so that the individual zealots of the "national spirit" do not become completely confused.

And one more particular remark, if one may say so. Some of the articles on the subjects we have discussed cannot be said to lack talent; they are written not without passion, they are polemically keen. It is only a pity that they defend a cause that lacks promise, a cause doomed to failure, being repudiated by life itself.

As is well known, Communist ideology expresses the ideals and aspirations of the working class, a class that is internationalist by nature. This is the reason that nationalism is incompatible with Soviet patriotism and proletarian internationalism, and is profoundly hostile to them. We regard instruction in patriotism first and foremost as instruction in Soviet patriotism, instruction in great pride in the social reality that has been created by labor and the struggle of generations of revolutionaries.

It is precisely in Marxism-Leninism as a revolutionary doctrine of the proletariat that the supreme spiritual values of humanity are embodied. As far as the past is concerned, the genuinely democratic, revolutionary elements and traditions in the nation's history are precious above all to us. We see the moral example not in the "lives of saints," not in embellished biographies of tsars and khans, but in the revolutionary heroic deed of the fighters for the people's happiness. We cherish everything created over centuries by the genius, mind, and labor of the people, but our pride is especially aroused by our present-day socialist reality.

Document 2

The Memorandum of December 1985[*]

The Imperative of Political Development

The practical and, even more, the potential progressiveness of socialism as a social structure is beyond dispute. Socialism has demonstrated its economic and social viability despite all the burdens of history and social cataclysms that have given birth to certain departures from the ideal.

But life, time, events give rise to paradoxes, which sometimes are unimaginable and absurd. If one takes a look at our society, the heroism of its course is obvious; more than that—it is startling. The selflessness, the beauty, the enthusiasm fused in a single surge gave birth to a living organism, which enjoys an enormous reserve of viability.

But all this has also given rise to enhanced demands on this society that is convinced it can conquer any heights and bear any burdens. The reckoning of unavoidable socioeconomic limitations somehow got lost in the storm of passions and events. If one adds to the objective factors the mistakes, the trials, the failures and breakdowns, then the resulting march of events has formed a real society, teeming with real life, that absorbed victories and defeats, successes and failures, luck and misfortunes, enthusiasm and expectations, satisfaction with what had been achieved and demands to move forward faster.

For some, the complications of the advance have caused depression, for others disappointment; they have led yet others to the striving for an alternative (not necessarily one based on private property), and yet in others to the belief in the inevitability of new measures that would strengthen the party, the state, socialism. The mosaic is rich and spacious, and this is normal.

---

[*] *Perestroika*, 28–38.

However, in any event, for one reason or others, along with the country's consolidation a dangerous process *of social disaffection* develops among diverse strata of society. The causes and the range of claims are diverse, but the process itself is clear. There is a need for real measures to unite society on a new basis. The old one is in some measure eroded. The new one is only being created. The month of April marked but the beginning of hopes, but its very mood reflected anxiety over what was happening. Life is pulling society into the era of inevitable changes. Every delay, even if an unconscious one, spells ruin. Besides, the political string is so taut that a rupture can be very painful.

I. The Objective: Man

In all his mutual relations and manifestations—production, society, politics, culture, way of life, interests, psychology, health, etc. *This is socialism—not in slogans but in practice.*

II. The Ultimate Result

The strengthening and development of socialism, the strengthening and development of the party and state, the enhancement of the attractiveness of the new order.

III. The Means

Today the problem is not economics—this is but the material basis of the process. The crux is in the political system, or rather, in its workings, its movement, its track to humans, its relationship to man, in the degree of its serving role. From which follows the necessity:

1. Of a rapprochement between the practice of socialism and its ideal, the elimination of the breach between word and deed. The ever-closer merger of the interests of the individual, groups, society as a whole.

2. Of consistent and complete democratism (at every stage, in accord with the concrete historical possibilities).

3. Of the development of the individual as an independent, creative, conscious force, united with others in its thoughts and actions. The transformation of every human into a genuine master of the country. The real involvement of one and all in the perfectibility of life, locally and in the state as a whole. This is the main point on which depends the solution of the first two. Here lies the basis of the liquidation of social discontent, insofar as, first, the people will themselves notice the positive changes, the tempo of which will considerably quicken, and second, acquiring responsibility along with rights, they will see what today is real and what is not. Third, not someone "from the top" but they themselves, the masses, will be responsible for everything that transpires, including whatever is unrealized and omitted.

One of the most important conditions (and also aspects) of the process of genuine development of the masses as actual and formal masters of the country entails the transformation of every human being into a personality (*lichnost'*) who stands consciously on the socialist terrain and is in command of at least the rudiments of the dialectical-materialistic method of thinking (the unchaining of thought!) without which the development of his creative character is unattainable.

Thus, the cementing of society takes place not only by external hoops, by forces external to the human being, but from within, when everyone is consciously and purposefully merged with all the others, [and] in constant and active interaction with them.

IV. The Principles of the Process

1. Enhancing the dynamism of society by means of a fuller utilization of the advantages of the system, the development of its Communist nature. The growth of the competitive ability (including moral-psychological ability) in the struggle of the two systems, the parallel development of the humanitarian advantages of socialism. In the forefront ever more clearly emerges

the problem of the position and role of the individual in society, the individual's relationship with other individuals. In a certain sense, socialism and democracy are identical, because it is precisely under socialism that democracy, in the broad sense of this word, is *concurrently the means and the goal of the movement.* In fact we are democratic, but in form often anti-democratic. To bring the form in accord with the content, the content of today and tomorrow.

Socialism is a more diverse system, providing alternative choices and, in particular, for this reason a system that is by its nature profoundly democratic, because democracy is above all the freedom (even in the capacity of realized necessity) of choice. But with us, there is the absence of alternative, there is centralization. *We have, as if, suppressed the dialectic of contradictions and want to develop only one of its aspects.*

The absence of choice in all realms and all phases (the Asiatic past, the history of the country in general, capitalist encirclement, etc.). Presently, we, on the whole, do not understand the essence of the approaching and historically inevitable transition from the time when there was no choice or when choice was historically impossible, to the time when, without democratic choice in which each person participates, it will be impossible to develop successfully. Meanwhile, the absence of *a socialist alternative* induces a search for it outside, and a certain part of the population finds it in one or another aspect of the bourgeois system.

There should be *freedom of choice,* but *exclusively and fully on a socialist basis.*

2. The *comprehensiveness* of reforming *all aspects of life*— from the economy to "formal," external features of democracy.

3. *The simultaneity* or even the anticipatory pace in key spheres (above all, in the party).

4. *Decisiveness* limited only by the real (if there will be such) dangers of the subversion of the foundations of socialism and the reduction of the might of the party and the state as a foreign policy factor (chiefly). Inside the country, the retention of sufficient strength (in coordination with foreign policy tasks),

taking into account the process of gradual—even if in distant perspective—withering of a series of state functions. Where possible and necessary—experiment of local (in space and time) significance.

5. The very process should be directed not only from above but also from below, by the hands of the masses, while the party directs and instructs them in democratic as well as consciously-socialist forms of existence and thought. "Democracy ought to become a habit" (Lenin).

6. Mobilizing the resources of science in the development of the process of democratization and control its interim results.

V. The Means

"Every step that takes us forward, higher in the task of developing productive forces and culture, should be accompanied by completing and altering our Soviet system" (Lenin).

1. *The initial moment*: a change in the methods of managing society by the party, which should mean the strengthening of its real power.

A change in the relationship between party and state power, between party and state organs, to the advantage of the state in form and in substance, and to the advantage of the party in substance.

The enhancement of the role of the state due to the necessity of further executive and economic centralization (in strategic sectors) and, concurrently, decentralization, as well as the raising of the masses' creative activity. The latter should be and can influence all-national processes, above all, by their direct and mediated control over the activity of the state through their influence on the state, its organs in the center and especially in the localities. The Council of Ministers is remote; hence the role of the region, the oblast [district], and other units. Under these conditions, the people's creativity in the removal of shortcomings, in the development of the socialist and Communist nature of society, will definitely rise.

From this follows a more clear-cut distribution of obligations, rights, and responsibilities between the party and the state. The party needs only to *direct* the fundamental tendencies of development and *control* them. First and foremost, it should be freed from purely economic, organizational, and supply functions (putting the idea crudely: at some stage to liquidate the sectoral, economic departments of party organs with all the ensuing consequences.) The party should be left only to deal with politics, the determination of the basic principles of economic and social policy. This is the main means of *control*. According to Lenin, the party's leadership of state organs should have a *political character*. The leading role of the party lies not in the substitution for the state and economic apparatus, but in constructive control.

To lead people, society through people, through one's "protégés." *The cadres are entirely in the hands of the party.* The political evaluation of their activity, and consequently their personal evaluation, belongs to party organizations.

The Central Committee should have only the following departments:

1. Economic policy
2. Social policy (including detection of social situations and opinions)
3. Ideological
4. Cadres and organizations
5. International
6. General

Internal party democracy should develop at a faster pace with respect to the other spheres of social life. Open admission into the party. Periodic accounting by Communists at open meetings of their work, something of a reattestation.

A system of evaluation and promotion of personnel, beginning with the election of lower party organizations. Not to impose leaders from above. To teach people from personal experience to evaluate and promote leaders. This alone will generate a healthy critical basis, the spirit of genuine party partisanship, adherence to party principles, and responsibility. Assuring within the party a real opportunity to express one's views. *Genuine clash of opinions, of discussion, along with unity of action* in the execution of adopted resolutions.

Introduce the system of preliminary evaluation of candidates for high positions directly in primary organizations or at meetings of their representatives (for all elective posts in district committees, city committees, oblast committees). Replacement of cadres. Age limit for leaders (guarantee of advisor-type job assignment). This applies not only to the sphere of party life but also to the soviet and economic spheres.

Full transparency of incomes. Many people favor maximum and minimum levels of wages for party and state leaders. The party and other personnel drawing closer to the masses' way of life. A single system of distribution instead of a separate one for each group of workers. A single system of wages for labor. Liquidation of castes: the state bureaucracy, the party machine, the military, intellectuals, technocracy, writers, artists, and others.

Membership in the party ought not to be a means of making a career. Presently, for many *who enroll in the party, the ideological factor has quite a formal meaning.*

It may be that at a certain stage it will be necessary to carry out a purge of the party in order to be rid of elements who compromise it. In any event, even now it is necessary to seek forms of influencing party members in the sense of making them maximally active.

3. *The division of functions* between the various parts of the system of administration will compel one part to nudge another. In particular, it is necessary to *change the relationship between the legislative and executive branches*, between the Supreme Soviet and the Council of Ministers, between the corresponding lower units. Presently, the former is stifled by the latter. The legislative organs merely discuss, and in practice decisions are made by the executive (i.e., they make decisions and do not simply execute).

It may be that a permanent parliamentary apparatus (not necessarily the continuing general session) will somewhat change the relations between the authorities. The binding force of the decisions taken by the legislative organs. Votes of confidence. It is necessary to sharply enhance the responsibility of executive authority to the legislative.

To change the practice of discussions, which at present bear the character of reports. They are necessary but ought to be *problematic*. To deal with new problems that confront the country, parliamentary commissions, etc., must be formed. *The functioning parliament*, which deals with the daily life of the country instead of ceremonially considering two or three questions: the plan, the budget, the international situation.

To define *the rights* of the deputies to the Supreme Soviet of the Soviet Union and of other deputies, especially at the local level. In particular, perhaps, the right of *energetic* interference, with the setting of *time limits* on the response of the relevant authorities of government.

Elections ought to be not a vote for one candidate but a choice, and the choice of the better [candidate]. One can limit the number of the nominated candidates (but to no fewer than two). Party control over nomination but not strict regulation, which has been discussed for a long time openly by everyone: "apportionment" (so many women, so many non-party members, so many manual workers, etc.).

The deputy ought to depend on the voters, with his lips truly expressing their opinions, and not his own opinion in their name. "We can govern only when we correctly express what the people are conscious of" (Lenin).

Accountability and changeability of deputies. Genuine recall of deputies—with publication, explanations. "More complete democracy by virtue of less formality, greater ease of election and recall" (Lenin).

Consequences: a colossal growth of real responsibility toward the masses, subordination, accountability, and, most importantly: the genuine involvement of the masses in the administration of regional, provincial, republican, and national affairs through direct and organized collective influence on the deputy. This will be especially effective in *the transformation of local soviets into genuine organs of authority*.

4. *Exhaustive glasnost'*: "The state is strong only when the masses know everything, when they can judge everything and are prepared to do everything consciously" (Lenin). *Glasnost'*, exhaustive and operative information, is an indispensable condition of the further democratization of social life. Only an informed person is capable of participating in the affairs of society with initiative and fruitfulness. It is senseless to summon to civil activity people who do not dispose of extensive information and are not placed in a favorable social climate for such creative activity.

In this same connection, one remark about ideological work. The causes that seriously lower the efficacy of the process of instruction exceed the bounds of ideological work itself.

Until now the principal point of departure of ideological activity has remained faulty. We continue to regard propaganda, that is, as the product of our consciousness—the book, the lecture, the play, the film, the address, the political instruction network—as the decisive condition of forming a socialist consciousness. Possibly this was highly important when the party was not in power. But is it not the consciousness of the propagandist, the writer, and the like that forms the consciousness of the people when it is in power? *Consciousness is formed by social life, in the process of political actions, the political movement of the mass itself.* On this subject there are numerous concrete pronouncements by V. I. Lenin, who emphasized that it was "not some studies or books and such," not speeches and rallies, but "political actions," "participation in the daily real struggle," "*one's own political experience . . . of the masses*"—this is what is the determining, decisive, principal condition of the Communist *education of the people, the forming of its socialist consciousness.* And this is the realm not of ideology but of democracy—soviet, socialist democracy.

5. *Real independence of the judiciary authority from all other branches of power.* There exists a dangerous opinion that we have no justice. In fact it is one of the most transparent forms of power.

The independence of the judge, real guarantees of independence in the principles of the judicial organization, the procedure of recall, etc.

The permanence of the judge—recall only under defined conditions. But with us it is a five years' term. The closer the date of the elections, the less there is adherence to principle. It is no accident that there is incessant reshuffling of judges. Raise the term to ten years at least, stabilize the status of the judge. Judiciary enterprise ought to be a profession.

Presently there are more than enough of those who want to meddle with the administration of justice. One should treat such interference and settlement of concrete cases as a crime, punishable according to law.

The criminal code—firmness, stability. Inevitability and severity of punishments of anti-social elements, especially for thieves, no mercy for murderers.

And along with this—real guarantees of securing the rights of the individual. There should be a law about human rights and their guarantees, a law about the inviolability of persons, property and residence, about the privacy of correspondence, telephone conversations, private life.

Organizational forms of achieving the right to demonstrate, freedom of speech, freedom of conscience, of the press, of assembly, of relocation.

We want everyone to have great civic responsibilities, but this is possible only if there are great civil rights.

6. *The broadest judicial protection of the rights of the individual* on every issue, including appeals against the actions of government organs. The citizen ought to have the right to bring a suit against a public official and an organization. There must be administrative courts for the settlement of conflicts in administrative cases.

Law and *by-laws*, normative acts. Law ought to have a mandatory character. And with us laws are plans, budgets, which are far from being fully enacted. Perhaps this ought not to have the status of law? The office of the public prosecutor, which in principle ought to supervise the execution of the law, is in fact idle. Even the ministers, not to speak of the Council of Ministers, for the most part, violate the laws with their instructions and directives.

A person should have assurance that his needs and complaints will be loyally and operatively dealt with by competent individuals and authorities. Presently, no one is ever punished for an *unlawful refusal*. But for *a lawful permission* they do punish. For this reason, it has become established: first refuse, then lodge an appeal, then, perhaps, decide positively. Red tape: time and the nerves of people are *spent on nothing*. An atmosphere of discontent emerges. What if one were to conduct sociological studies of the number of refusals and then of received permissions?

Responsibility ought to be correctly distributed and *officials should bear responsibility for dodging it*. Briefly: an individual must respect the state, but the state is no less obliged to respect the individual. Otherwise there will always be a barrier between them, and even a rupture. It is necessary to secure constitutionally *the responsibilities of the state toward the citizen*.

The coordination of authority within the judiciary system. The courts on all levels occupy themselves only with justice, and the remaining functions pertain to the Ministry of Justice. Thus it was under Lenin. The Supreme Court or the State Council, which would decide the constitutionality of various acts, of their conformity to the nature of socialism. The full independence of the Supreme Court from all pressure.

7. "We are unable even to conceive accurately at the present time . . . which forces stay unused and can unfold under the socialist system. Our task is only to clear the path for all these forces" (Lenin). A most important role in this clearance of the socialist potential belongs to economic policy. Underestimation of its possibilities and significance will prolong stagnation.

On this path [lies] *the profound democratization of economic life*. It is vitally essential to speed up economic development significantly. But this cannot be done by scientific-technical and economic means alone. It is necessary to involve and fully unfold moral and psychological factors. And this requires extensive democracy in the economy, combined with its centralized state administration.

"Every democracy, as in general, every political superstructure (unavoidable until the complete elimination of classes, until there is created a classless society), in the last analysis serves production and is determined, in the final analysis, by the productive relations of the society in question" (Lenin).

Interaction of democracy and economy. "Taken separately, no democracy produces socialism, but in real life, democracy will not be 'taken separately' but 'jointly,' exerting its influence also on the economy, nudging its transformation, subjecting itself to the influence of economic development, etc. Such is the dialectic of live history" (Lenin).

Real participation of the masses in planning, administration, realization. The creation of a single positive and self-developing basis—genuine, organic, consistent unity of the interests of the individual, the collective, and society. All the potentials of economic democratization inhere in the nature of socialism.

Perhaps one should consider organizations like "workers' councils"? Evidently, if correctly interpreted, this idea is not so "dangerous." Labor democracy not in the Trotskyist sense. (Lenin opposed only attempts to contrast democracy with one-man management in the production process.) The rights of the collective, including in relation to the managers of enterprises, are far from anarcho-syndicalism. In this, not only the director but also the collective will bear responsibility for the enterprise, for its work.

Economic relations and *liability!*—direct, severe, material. The right to economic initiative not only for collectives but also for the individual (experience, socioeconomic experiment, for example, in the sphere of consumer service). Concerns and trusts operating on a fully self-supporting basis.)

Perhaps one should consider basing the entire system of consumers' service and trade on cooperative principles. The state fixes the prices and credits them to pay for the premises and facilities. There ought to be a choice between two or three stores, laundries, etc.

It is necessary to have a code of economic law, but only if the contracting parties are independent. We need an up-to-date Labor Law Code (KZOT). Ours is antediluvian.

To curb the Ministry of Finances, which, in the pursuit of

today's kopeika deprives society of tomorrow's hundreds and thousands of rubles. Liquidate financial arbitrariness. Introduce fixed norms of payments and the enterprises' income charges.

Transformation of the monopoly of foreign trade—decisive integration with socialist countries (as the initial phase).

Trade unions at the present time play in many respects a formal role. Their importance should be sharply raised. They should be given more serious functions than the collection of dues and the distribution of sanatorium vouchers (of course, to put the whole matter roughly). Politically, we will gain.

VI. The Way Out—The Principal Decision

No matter how we improve this or that sphere, sector, part of the mechanism, or general coordination, there will be no benefit from mere improvement. And what is most important: there will be no self-motion, no sort of "self-liquidation" of shortcomings, no supremacy of common sense, no elimination or reduction of the bureaucracy's dictatorship. If one is to talk seriously about the creativity of the people, about the sovereignty of its power expressed through the party, the state, or social organizations, then it is necessary, absolutely necessary, to organize matters in such a way that on the principle of the inviolability of party leadership, especially on its highest level, the masses are involved in the process of political actions, political decisions.

To this end adopt the following principal scheme of leadership:

1. The supreme party and state power is realized by the *President of the USSR.*

He is also chairman of the Communist Union (Union of Communists) of the USSR, chairman of the United Politburo of the Party, which constitutes the Communist Union; and chairman of the Council of the Presidents of the Republics.

2. The president is elected for a period of 10 years on the basis of direct national elections from among candidates nominated by parties that constitute the *Union of Communists.*

3. The Union of Communists consists of two parties: Socialist and National-Democratic. General elections—every 5 years—from top to bottom.

The Union of Communists has a common (general) charter; the parties have more detailed charters.

4. The president has two vice presidents: from the party, the chairman of *KPK** (a disciplinary and conciliatory organ); from the state, the chairman of the Committee of National Control.

The president has corresponding secretaries (for the party and the state), including a group of advisors on national security.

5. The government is headed by the general secretary of the party that has won the nationwide elections.

6. The question of the work and functions of the Supreme Soviet is separate, subject to further deliberations. Here there can be many variants, but this is a matter of consequence, not of principle.

All this, taken together, will solve many problems, which in any event will have to be solved, but it is better to anticipate them. This will be a revolutionary perestroika of a *historic nature*. The pressure of time's demands is weakened. Such questions as the activity of the individual, the change of personnel, the struggle against inertia, etc., will be solved without special expenses. The political culture of society will grow, and this means that so also will real stability.

---

* The acronym stands for *Komitet Partiinogo Kontroliia* [Committee of Party Control].

Acknowledgments

I WOULD LIKE to express my profound gratitude to Mr. Anatoly Yakovlev, Alexander's son, for the help he has given me. He answered many questions, corrected many mistakes, and provided me with most of the illustrations. His assistance was invaluable. I also wish to thank Professor and Mrs. Jiri Valenta for giving me access to their unpublished interview with Alexander Yakovlev and offering useful suggestions. Mr. Evgenii Efremov has provided me with a variety of sources.

Richard Pipes

Illustrations

Unless otherwise identified, all illustrations are courtesy of Mr. Anatoly Yakovlev.

Frontispiece: Alexander Yakovlev

Following Page 38

In front of school with cousins, Konstantin and Nikolai, 1931. Alexander is on the right.

In military school, January, 1942.

Yakovlev's parents, September, 1976.

With wife and daughter, Natasha.

Columbia University, 1959. Yakovlev is on the extreme right. Oleg Kalugin is second from left. From Oleg Kalugin, *Spy Master* (London, 1994).

In conversation with E. E. Ligachev and Mikhail Gorbachev (on the right).

As Soviet Ambassador to Canada introduced to the Canadian Governor General, 1977. From *Aleksandr Iakovlev: Svoboda— moia religiia* (Moscow, 2003).

Walking with Gorbachev, possibly on Canadian Minister Whelan's farm, during their historic encounter, May 1983.

Anti-Yakovlev demonstration in Moscow, February, 1991. The sign—"Promakha ne budet"—means "We shall not miss."

Recipient of honorary degree from Exeter University in the United Kingdom, 1993. From *Aleksandr Iakovlev: Svoboda— moia religiia.*

Abbreviations of Yakovlev's Works

Gor'kaia chasha: Gor'kaia chasha: Bol'shevizm i Reformatsiia
Rossii [The Bitter Cup: Bolshevism and the
Reformation of Russia]

Interv'iu: Izbrannye interv'iu, 1992–2005, in *Rossiia:
XX vek* [Selected Interviews, 1992–2005]

Krestosev: Krestosev [The Sowing of Crosses]

Muki: Muki prochteniia bytiia—perestroika:
nadezdy i real'nosti [The Torments of
Reading Being—Perestroika; Hopes and
Realities]

Omut: Omut pamiati ot Stolypina do Putina, 2 vols.
[The Whirlpool of Memory from Stolypin to
Putin]

Perestroika: Perestroika, 1985–1991, in *Rossiia: XX vek*
[Reconstruction, 1895–1991]

Po moshcham: Po moshcham i elei: Avtorskaia redaktsiia
[On Relics and Unctions: Author's Editon]

Predislovie: Predislovie, Obval, Posleslovie [Introduction,
Avalanche, Afterword]

Realizm: Realizm—zemlia perestroiki [Realism—The
Soil of Reconstruction]

Sumerki: Sumerki [Twilight]

Notes

Notes to Preface

1. *Interv'iu*, 310.
2. Michael Dobbs, *Down with Big Brother* (New York, 1997), 178.
3. Gerd Ruge, *Gorbachev: A Biography* (London, 1991), 128.
4. *Interv'iu*, 183.
5. Mikhail Gorbachev, *Memoirs* (New York, 1996), 459; *Kommersant*, October 19, 2005 (no. 197/3,281).

Notes to Chapter One

1. *Muki*, 50.
2. Ibid., 28.
3. Bill Keller in *New York Times Magazine*, February 19, 1989.
4. *Muki*, 28.
5. *Sumerki*, 41; *Muki*, 47–48.
6. *Omut*, 1:34.
7. *Muki, 28.*
8. *Omut*, 1:25.
9. *Muki*, 63.
10. *Omut*, 1:25, 28–29; Dusko Doder and Louise Branson, *Gorbachev: Heretic in the Kremlin* (New York, 1990), 97.
11. Doder and Branson, *Gorbachev*, 97.
12. *Omut*, 1:29.
13. *Muki*, 48.

Notes to Chapter Two

1. *Interv'iu*, 127.
2. Christopher Shulgan, *The Soviet Ambassador* (Toronto, 2008), 27.
3. *Interv'iu*, 87.
4. Ibid., 378.
5. *Omut*, 1:54-55.
6. Ibid., 54.
7. *Gor'kaia chasha*, 9.
8. *Interv'iu*, 174.
9. *Omut*, 1:58; *Interv'iu*, 277.
10. *Interv'iu*, 163.
11. *Gor'kaia chasha*, 10.
12. *Muki*, 51.

Notes to Chapter Three

1. *Omut*, 1:169.
2. *Sumerki*, 254-55.
3. *Interv'iu*, 363.
4. *Gor'kaia chasha*, 154. It was first published in Russia in April 1989 in *News of the Central Committee of the Communist Party of the Soviet Union*: Anatol Shub in *The New Leader*, July-August 2002, p. 21.
5. *Krestosev*, 9.
6. Ibid., 10
7. *Predislovie*, 5.
8. *Perestroika*, 664.
9. Ibid., 664-65.
10. *Interv'iu*, 309.
11. Alexander Yakovlev, interview by Jiri and Leni Valenta, Moscow, September 28, 2000, recounted in their unpublished manuscript *Russia's Democratic Revolution*.

Notes to Chapter Four

1. *Interv'iu*, 113.
2. Bill Keller, "Moscow's Other Mastermind," *New York Times Magazine*, February 19, 1989.
3. The casual diary notes he made while at Columbia are available on the internet at http://www.alexanderyakovlev/personal-archive/lifedoc-doc/1000042/1000043 and 1000047.
4. Loren R. Graham, *Moscow Stories* (Bloomington, IN, 2006), 224; Gail Sheehy, *Gorbachev: The Making of the Man Who Shook the World* (London, 1991), 302.
5. *Sumerki*, 334.
6. *Strelka*, reproduced at http://www.alexanderyakovlev.org/personal-archive/lifedoc-doc/1000042/1000047.
7. *Interv'iu*, 6; *Omut*, 1:278, 280.
8. *Daily Talking*, April 12, 2009. http://www.dailytalking.ru/interview/yakovlev-aleksandr-nikolaevich/105.
9. *Omut*, 1:283.

Notes to Chapter Five

1. *Sumerki*, 324.
2. *Omut*, 1:272.
3. Igor Zabelin, *Chelovek i chelovechestvo* (Moscow, 1970), 166.
4. Leonid Mlechin, *Gorbachev i El'tsin* (Moscow, 2012), 147.
5. *Pravda*, November 25, 1972 (no. 330/19,838), p. 3.
6. *Sumerki*, 274.

7. Ibid., 325.

8. Bill Keller, "Moscow's Other Mastermind," *New York Times Magazine,* February 19, 1989. See also *Interv'iu,* 6–7.

9. *Muki,* 62.

10. *Interv'iu,* 191.

Notes to Chapter Six

1. Shulgan, *Soviet Ambassador,* 175.

2. Ibid., 172.

3. *Omut,* 1:245-46.

4. *Perestroika,* 62.

5. See p. 24.

6. *Sumerki,* 340.

7. Ibid., 349, 356.

8. Ibid., 356.

9. *Interv'iu,* 337.

10. *Muki,* 353.

11. Gorbachev, *Memoirs,* 148.

12. Shulgan, *Soviet Ambassador,* 248–50.

13. Mlechin, *Gorbachev i El'tsin,* 148.

14. "Shaping Russia's Transformation: A Leader of Perestroika Looks Back: Interview with Alexander Yakovlev." Institute of International Studies at the University of California, Berkeley, November 21, 1996.

15. Shulgan, *Soviet Ambassador,* 267.

16. *Muki,* 354.

17. Petr Cherkasov, *IMEMO* (Moscow, 2004), 532.

18. Keller in *New York Times Magazine,* February 19, 1989.

19. *Aleksandr Iakovlev: Svoboda—moia religiia,* 88.

20. *Gor'kaia chasha,* 13.

21. *Omut,* 1:345.

22. Yakovlev admitted authorship in *Muki,* 62–63. The pseudonym seems to be a play on his mother's name, Agafiia.

23. *Bednyi Santa Klaus,* 3–5.

24. Ibid., 93.

25. *Muki,* 63. In 1978, Canada expelled eleven Soviet diplomats on charges of spying.

Notes to Chapter Seven

1. *Muki,* 365; *Sumerki,* 361.

2. Stephen F. Cohen and Katrina Vanden Heuvel, *Voices of Glasnost* (New York, 1989), 35.

3. Cherkasov, *IMEMO,* 525.

4. Ibid., 534-35.

5. *Omut,* 1:345-46.

6. Mlechin, *Gorbachev i El'tsin,* 149.

7. *Omut,* 1:349.

8. *Perestroika,* 775. Reagan had extended similar invitations to Gorbachev's immediate predecessors, K. U. Chernenko and Iu. V. Andropov. Neither led to a meeting. Ibid.

9. Ibid., 12.

10. Ibid.

11. A. N. Yakovlev, *Ot Trumena do Reigana* (Moscow, 1984), 14, 98.

12. Jonathan Harris, "The Public Politics of Aleksandr Nikolaevich Yakovlev, 1983–1989," *The Carl Beck Papers in Russian and East European Studies,* no. 901 (1990): 16.

Notes to Chapter Eight

1. *Sumerki,* 28.

2. Ibid., 383.

3. *Interv'iu,* 48.

4. *Omut,* 1:17.

5. *Interv'iu,* 309.

6. Dobbs, *Down with Big Brother,* 197–98.

Notes to Chapter Nine

1. There is a lengthy essay by Yakovlev on Gorbachev in *Omut,* 2:5–85.

2. *Sumerki,* 463.

3. *Interv'iu,* 203, 205.

4. *Sumerki,* 476.

5. Shulgan, *Soviet Ambassador,* 280; *Omut,* 2:8.

6. *Pravda,* October 21, 1986, no. 294 (24,916), p. 1.

7. Sheehy, *Gorbachev,* 205–06.

8. Anatoly S. Chernyaev, *My Six Years with Gorbachev* (University Park, PA, 2000), 245–46.

9. Valery Boldin, *Ten Years That Shook the World* (New York, 1994), 160.

10. Timothy J. Colton, *Yeltsin: A Life* (New York, 2008), 207.

Notes to Chapter Ten

1. *Omut,* 1:383.

2. David Remnick, *Lenin's Tomb* (New York, 1993), 297.

3. *Perestroika,* 789.

4. Stephen White, *Gorbachev and After* (Cambridge, 1991), 86-88.

5. *Omut,* 1:21.

6. Yitzhak M. Brudny, *Reinventing Russia* (Cambridge, 1998), 197.

7. R. G. Pikhoia, *Sovetskii Soiuz: Istoriia vlasti, 1945–1991* (Moscow, 1998), 504-05.

8. An extensive list of such works can be found in chapter 3 of Stephen White's, *Gorbachev and After*.

9. David Wedgwood Benn, *From Glasnost to Freedom of Speech* (London, 1992) 17–19.

10. *Perestroika*, 493–94.

11. *Interv'iu*, 209; Archie Brown, *The Gorbachev Factor* (Oxford, 1996), 164–65.

12. Mikhail Gorbachev, *Naedine s soboi* (Moscow, 2012), 439.

Notes to Chapter Eleven

1. *Predislovie*, 266; see also Brown, *The Gorbachev Factor*, 95.

2. *Omut*, 1:413.

Notes to Chapter Twelve

1. Gorbachev, *Memoirs*, 459.

2. Sheehy, *Gorbachev*, 187.

3. Dobbs, *Down with Big Brother*, 288.

4. *Perestroika*, 377–78.

5. Dobbs, *Down with Big Brother*, 199; Shulgan, *Soviet Ambassador*, 97; E. K. Ligachev, *Zagadka Gorbacheva* (Novosibirsk, 1992), 137–40.

6. *Omut*, 1:276–79.

7. Ibid., 281.

8. *Znanie-sila*, no. 12 (2003), 16–17.

9. Jiri and Leni Valenta, interview with Yakovlev on September 28, 2000.

10. See p. 51.

11. White, *Gorbachev and After*, 85.

12. *Perestroika*, 380–81.

13. Dobbs, *Down with Big Brother*, 178; Robert G. Kaiser, *Why Gorbachev Happened* (New York, 1991), 121.

14. The National Security Archive, http://www.gwu.edu/-nsarchiv/NSAEBB/NSAEBB168, Document 3.

Notes to Chapter Thirteen

1. Sheehy, *Gorbachev*, 331.

2. White, *Gorbachev and After*, 85.

3. *Voprosy istorii*, no. 6 (1989): 20.

4. *Perestroika*, 345.

5. *Omut*, 2:251. The text of the speech is in *Realizm*, 518–34.

6. *Perestroika*, 348.

7. *Omut*, 1:417.

8. *Realizm*, 533.

Notes to Chapter Fourteen

1. Jeane J. Kirkpatrick, *The Withering Away of the Totalitarian State . . . and Other Surprises* (Washington, DC, 1990), 40.
2. Remnick, *Lenin's Tomb*, 296.
3. *Omut*, 1:350.
4. *Prizyv ubivat': Amerikanskie falsifikatory problem voiny i mira* (Moscow, 1965), 3.
5. *Literaturnaia gazeta*, June 26, 1985.
6. *Ot Trumena do Reigana*, passim.
7. A. N. Yakovlev, ed., *Ialtinskaia konferentsiia 1945: Uroki istorii* (Moscow, 1985), 6.
8. *Omut*, 1:377.
9. *Interv'iu*, 347.
10. Ibid.
11. Ibid., 174.
12. *Perestroika*, 42, 43, 52.
13. Ibid., 159-64 and 166-71.
14. *Gor'kaia chasha*, 182.
15. *Interv'iu*, 245.

Notes to Chapter Fifteen

1. *Perestroika*, 37.
2. *Omut*, 1:423.
3. Gorbachev, *Memoirs*, 318.
4. Ibid., 323.

Notes to Chapter Sixteen

1. *Perestroika*, 787, and Dobbs, *Down with Big Brother*, 203.
2. Gyorgy Dalos, *Gorbatschow: Mensch und Macht* (Munich, 2011), 172.
3. Nina Andreeva in *The Current Digest of the Soviet Press* 40, no. 14, April 27, 1988, 1-6.
4. *Omut*, 2:231-35; and *Perestroika*, 192–200.
5. *Omut*, 1:438.
6. Ibid., 439–40.
7. *Po moshcham*, 110.
8. *Interv'iu*, 254.
9. *Omut*, 1:448.
10. *Perestroika*, 605.
11. Chernyaev, *My Six Years*, 111.
12. *Krestosev*, 229–44.
13. Andrei S. Grachev, *Final Days* (Boulder, CO, 1995), 29.
14. Oleg Kalugin, *Spy Master* (London, 1994), 241.

15. Mlechin, *Gorbachev i El'tsin*, 87.

16. *Interv'iu*, 61.

17. *Perestroika*, 633.

18. Vladimir Kriuchkov, *Lichnoe Delo* 1 (Moscow, 1996), 283.

19. *Perestroika*, 243–45.

20. *Omut*, 1:14.

21. *Kommersant*, March 14, 2000; *Omut*, 1:430; *Sumerki*, 472.

22. *Predislovie*, 6.

23. *Interv'iu*, 14.

24. *Omut*, 1:5.

25. Ibid., 1:431.

26. Ibid., 2:411–17.

27. *Daily Talking*, April 12, 2009. http://www.dailytalking.ru/interview/yakovlev-aleksandr-nikolaevich/105.

28. *Aleksandr Iakovlev: Svoboda—moia religiia*, 266-67; *Omut*, 2:397.

Notes to Chapter Seventeen

1. 197. *Reabilitatsiia: Politicheskie protsessy 30-50kh godov* (Moscow, 1991), 15, 17; *Omut*, 1:550.

2. *Daily Talking*, April 12, 2009. http://www.dailytalking.ru/interview/yakovlev-aleksandr-nikolaevich/105.

3. *Interv'iu*, 311, 314.

4. *Omut*, 1:9. Yakovlev credited the Russian Nobel Prize laureate Lev Landau with this idea: *Omut*, 1:550.

5. *Omut*, 1:9–10.

6. *Krestosev*, 23, 26.

7. *Interv'iu*, 224.

8. White, *Gorbachev and After*, 84.

9. It has been translated into English as *A Century of Violence in Soviet Russia* and published in 2002 by Yale University Press.

10. *Krestosev*, 268–70.

11. *Interv'iu*, 196.

12. *Omut*, 1:326.

13. They are the subject of my first book, *The Formation of the Soviet Union* (Cambridge, MA, 1954).

14. *Omut*, 1:618–21.

15. *Krestosev*, 3.

16. *Interv'iu*, 303.

Notes to Chapter Eighteen

1. Sheehy, *Gorbachev*, 430.

2. *Omut*, 2:406.

3. *Aleksandr Iakovlev: Svoboda—moia religiia*, 49.

Notes to Chapter Nineteen

1. Sheehy, *Gorbachev*, 413.
2. *Interv'iu*, 188.

Notes to Chapter Twenty

1. *Omut*, 2:307–10.
2. Ibid., 308.
3. *Perestroika*, 689.
4. *Omut*, 2:311.
5. Ibid., 1:429.
6. *Interv'iu*, 294.
7. Mikhail Gorbachev, *The August Coup* (London, 1991), 11.
8. *Perestroika*, 826.
9. *Interv'iu*, 23.
10. Shulgan, *Soviet Ambassador*, 294–97.
11. Ibid., 124.
12. Ibid., 257.

Notes to Chapter Twenty-One

1. Sheehy, *Gorbachev*, 318.
2. *Aleksandr Iakovlev: Svoboda—moia religiia*, 274–75.
3. *Omut*, 1:310.
4. *Interv'iu*, 184.
5. Ibid., 94.
6. Ibid., 94.
7. *Po moshcham*, 11.
8. *Interv'iu*, 31.

Notes to Chapter Twenty-Two

1. *Kommersant*, no. 197 (3,281), October 19, 2005.
2. Ibid.
3. *New York Times*, October 19, 2005, B8.
4. Boldin, *Ten Years that Shook the World*, 113.

Bibliography

Works of A. N. Yakovlev in Russian and English

Ideinaia nishcheta apologetov "kholodnoi voiny": Amerikanskaia burzhuaziia. Moscow, 1961.

Staryi mif v novom svete. Moscow, 1962.

Prizyv ubivat': Amerikanskie falsifikatory problem voiny i mira. Moscow, 1965.

Ideologiia amerikanskoi "imperii": Problemy voiny, mira i mezhdunarodnykh otnoshenii v poslevoennoi amerikanskoi burzhuaznoi literature. Moscow, 1967.

Pax Americana. Imperskaia ideologiia: Istoki doktriny. Moscow, 1969.

Bednyi Santa Klaus. Moscow, 1983. Published under the pseudonym N. Agashin.

Ot Trumena do Reigana: Doktriny i real'nosti iadernogo veka. Moscow, 1984. Translated as *On the Edge of an Abyss: From Truman to Reagan: The Doctrines and Realities of the Nuclear Age.* Moscow, 1985.

Soviet Society: Philosophy of Development. Moscow, 1988.

Realizm—zemlia perestroiki. Moscow, 1990.

Muki prochteniia byti'ia: Perestroika—nadezhdy i real'nosti. Moscow, 1991.

Na poroge XXI veka: Vystuplenie chlena Politicheskogo konsul'tativnogo komiteta pri Prezidente. Moscow, 1991.

Social Alternatives in the Twentieth Century. New York, 1992.

Predislovie—obval—posleslovie. Moscow, 1992. Translated as *The Fate of Marxism in Russia.* New Haven, 1993.

Gor'kaia chasha: Bol'shevizm i Reformatsiia Rossii. Iaroslavl, 1994.

Po moshcham i elei. Moscow, 1995.

K sotsial'noi demokratii. Moscow, 1996.

Postizhenie. Moscow, 1998.

Krestosev. Moscow, 2000. Translated as *A Century of Violence in Soviet Russia.* New Haven, 2002.

Omut pamiatii. 2 vols. Moscow, 2001.

Rossiia v nachale XX veka. Moscow, 2002.

Sumerki. Moscow, 2003.

Aleksandr Iakovlev: Svoboda—moia religiia. Moscow, 2003.

Perestroika, 1985–1991: Neizdannoe, neizvestnoe, zabytoe. Moscow, 2008.

Izbrannye interv'iu: 1992–2005. Moscow, 2009.

Works Edited by Alexander Yakovlev

SSha: Ot velikogo k bol'nomu. Moscow, 1969.

Osnovy politicheskikh znanii: Uchebnoe posobie. Moscow, 1973. Translated as *Fundamentals of Political Science.* Moscow, 1975.

Ialtynskaia konferentsiia 1945: uroki istorii. Moscow, 1985. Translated as *The Yalta Conference: The Lessons of History.* Moscow, 1985.

Kapitalizm na iskhode stoletiia. Moscow, 1987. Translated as *Capitalism at the End of the Century.* Moscow, 1988.

Reabilitatsiia: Politicheskie protsessy 30–50kh godov. Moscow, 1991.

Secondary Literature

Aron, Leon. *Yeltsin: A Revolutionary Life.* New York: 2000.

Benn, David Wedgwood. *From Glasnost to Freedom of Speech.* London: 1992.

Boldin, Valery. *Ten Years That Shook the World.* New York: 1994.

Brown, Archie. *The Gorbachev Factor.* Oxford: 1996.

Brudny, Yitzhak M. *Reinventing Russia.* Cambridge: 1998.

Cherkasov, P. P. *IMEMO.* Moscow: 2004.

Chernyaev, Anatolii. *My Six Years with Gorbachev.* University Park, PA, 2000.

Cohen, Stephen F., and Katrina Vanden Heuvel. *Voices of Glasnost.* New York, 1989.

Colton, Timothy J. *Yeltsin: A Life.* New York, 2008.

Dalos, Gyorgy. *Gorbatschow: Mensch und Macht.* Munich, 2011.

Dobbs, Michael. *Down with Big Brother.* New York, 1997.

Doder, Dusko, and Louise Branson. *Gorbachev: Heretic in the Kremlin.* New York, 1990.

Gorbachev, Mikhail. *The August Coup.* London, 1991.

———. *Memoirs.* New York, 1996.

———. *Naedine s Soboi.* Moscow, 2012.

Grachev, A. S. *Final Days.* Boulder, CO, 1995.

Graham, Loren. *Moscow Stories.* Bloomington, IN, 2006.

Kaiser, Robert G. *Why Gorbachev Happened.* New York, 1991.

Kalugin, Oleg. *The First Directorate.* New York, 1994.

Keller, Bill. "Moscow's Other Mastermind: Aleksandr Yakovlev, Gorbachev's Little-Known Alter-Ego." *New York Times Magazine.* February 19, 1989, 20ff.

Kirkpatrick, Jeane J. *The Withering Away of the Totalitarian State . . . and Other Surprises.* Washington, DC, 1990.

Kriuchkov, Vladimir. *Lichnoe Delo.* Moscow, 1996.

Ligachev, E. K. *Zagadka Gorbacheva.* Novosibirsk, 1992; published in English as *Inside Gorbachev's Kremlin: The Memoirs of Yegor Ligachev.* New York, 1993.

Mlechin, Leonid. *Gorbachev i El'tsin.* Moscow, 2012.

Remnick, David. *Lenin's Tomb.* New York, 1993.

Ruge, Gerd. *Gorbachev: A Biography.* London, 1991.

Sheehy, Gail. *Gorbachev: The Making of the Man Who Shook the World.* London, 1991.

Shulgan, Christopher. *The Soviet Ambassador.* Toronto, 2008.

White, Stephen. *Gorbachev and After.* Cambridge, 1991.

Index